DEATH
Investigators'
HANDBOOK

This book is dedicated to the investigator who

Knocks on one more door;
Misses one more hot meal;
Looks at the scene photographs one more time;
Makes one more phone call;
Makes one last try;

Solves one more case.

VOLUME ONE
Crime Scenes

DEATH
Investigator's
HANDBOOK

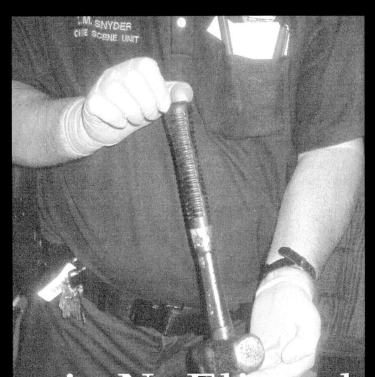

Louis N. Eliopulos
Paladin Press • Boulder, Colorado

Also by Louis N. Eliopulos:
Death Investigator's Handbook, Volume Two: Investigations
Death Investigator's Handbook, Volume Three: Scientific Investigations

Death Investigator's Handbook:
Volume One: Crime Scenes
by Louis N. Eliopulos

Copyright © 2003 by Louis N. Eliopulos

ISBN 13: 978-1-58160-496-2
Printed in the United States of America

Published by Paladin Press, a division of
Paladin Enterprises, Inc.
Gunbarrel Tech Center
7077 Winchester Circle
Boulder, Colorado 80301 USA
+1.303.443.7250

Direct inquiries and/or orders to the above address.

PALADIN, PALADIN PRESS, and the "horse head" design
are trademarks belonging to Paladin Enterprises and
registered in United States Patent and Trademark Office.

Visit our website at www.paladin-press.com

TABLE OF CONTENTS

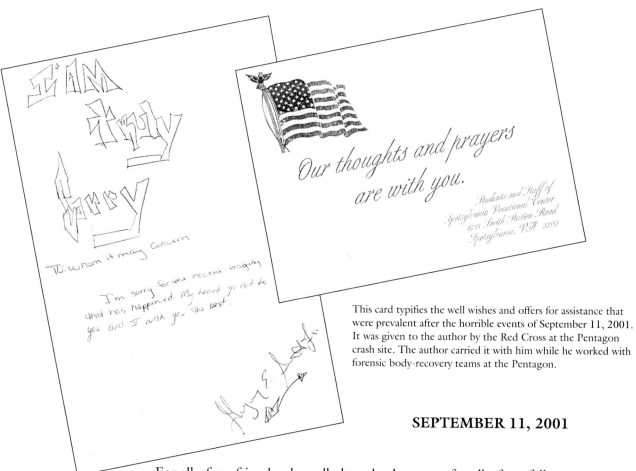

This card typifies the well wishes and offers for assistance that were prevalent after the horrible events of September 11, 2001. It was given to the author by the Red Cross at the Pentagon crash site. The author carried it with him while he worked with forensic body-recovery teams at the Pentagon.

SEPTEMBER 11, 2001

For all of my friends who called to check on me; for all of my fellow professionals who contacted me to volunteer their time and effort; for the homicide detective that called me and told me if it was his son who had died inside the Pentagon, he would want me to be the one to bring him out; for the school children who sent us notes and the people who brought flowers; for the Salvation Army and the Red Cross, which took care of our every want and need; to the church group from North Carolina who slept on the floor so that they could serve us hot meals—I say thank you.

Among the senseless tragedy and horrible carnage that occurred on September 11, 2001, I saw America at its very best. Deeply saddened, we collected our dead and grieved our terrible losses. And then, we moved on. I was never so proud to be an American. Your thoughts and prayers were not only heard but also deeply felt. I was so very proud to represent you.

—Lou Eliopulos
2003

ACKNOWLEDGMENTS

A very special thank-you for the continuous education and opportunity of working with the following true professionals of the forensic sciences:

Dr. Peter Lipkovic
Dr. Bonifacio Floro
Dr. William Maples
Dr. Arthur Burns
Dr. Margarita Arruza
Dr. Anthony Falsetti

Also, my profound appreciation to those individuals with whom I have shared the joy of solved cases and the agony and frustration of having a case remain unresolved:

Bruce Herring
William Hagerty
Dave Early
Tom Asimos
Robbie Hinson
Carol Dean
Pete Hughes
Jim Grebas
Mike Sullivan
Ralph Blincoe
Mark Fox
Sheri Blanton
Gerry Nance
Dayle Hinman
Dr. Jason Byrd
Brian Stamper

PUBLISHER'S NOTE

The contact information contained in this book was accurate at the time of publication.

CRIME SCENES

PART I

A good detective looks at the scene and comprehends the pieces as a part of the greater whole. He somehow manages to isolate the important details, to see those items which conform to the scene, those that conflict, and those that are inexplicably absent.

Whatever and whenever the scene, its value as a baseline for a murder investigation depends entirely on the detective—his ability to keep out the rabble and maintain the scene itself; his capacity for observation, for contemplating the scene in its totality, in its parts, and from every conceivable angle; his willingness to perform every task that could possibly yield evidence from a particular scene; his common sense in avoiding those procedures that would be meaningless or futile.

—David Simon, *Homicide, A Year on the Killing Streets*

CHAPTER 1: CRIME-SCENE INVESTIGATION

INITIAL SCENE PROTOCOL

1) Establish the crime scene perimeter.
    a) The area should be roped off and secured.
        i) Make sure sufficient boundaries are established.
            (1) Consider media and range of lenses and sound equipment used by the media.
            (2) Use tact in dealing with citizens.
                (a) Some citizens may end up being witnesses who have valuable information to add to the investigation.
                (b) In highly volatile areas or cases, onlookers could become irate to the point of interfering with the scene investigation.

2) Establish one route in and out of crime scenes.

3) Determine who has contaminated the crime scene.
    a) Check with rescue units.
    b) Check with responding police units.
    c) Interview all other persons who have been on the scene.
    d) Assign officers to guard the scene and record all persons coming and going.
        i) High-ranking officers can be a problem, so diplomacy must be used. Consider soliciting their help in preventing contamination.
        ii) Limit the number of persons at the scene in an effort to limit the number of prints found.
        iii) Remind officers of the possibility of their being involved in the chain of evidence. This may discourage contamination.
        iv) Be careful in allowing investigative team members to reenter the crime scene once they have left. Canvassing detectives may, unsuspecting, have become contaminated with trace evidence from a neighbor's residence. An astute defense attorney may later contend that evidence discovered at the scene implicating his client may have been brought to the crime scene by the canvassing detective reentering the crime scene after his neighborhood canvass.

4) Establish policy for crime-scene integrity.
    a) Water
    b) Lights
    c) Toilets
    d) Smoking
    e) Telephones
    f) Rubber gloves
    g) Film wrappers

5) Contact the necessary agencies to respond.
    a) Crime scene technicians
    b) Medical examiner personnel
    c) Prosecuting attorney

6) Evaluate the crime scene and consider whether specialized personnel are going to be needed before proceeding with the crime-scene search and examination.
    a) Anthropologist
    b) Bomb expert
    c) Blood-spatter expert
    d) Scuba divers

7) If scene is outdoors and at night, determine whether any special lighting will be required or, if possible, scene processing can be delayed until sunrise.

8) Photograph (and videotape if necessary) the entire scene before processing the scene.

BODY EXAMINATIONS

1) Begin examining the scene by starting with the body.

2) Make sure you describe what you see, not what you *think* you see.

3) Give a general description of the body.
    a) Clothing (style, color, unusual appearances such as tears, holes, pockets turned inside out, etc.)
    b) Location and appearance of wounds, bruises, foreign materials, etc.
    c) Blood
        i) Location
        ii) Patterns
        iii) Direction of flow
        iv) Degree of coagulation
    d) Condition, location, and extent of:
        i) Rigor mortis
        ii) Lividity
        iii) Other body conditions indicative of a time frame since death (consider taking atmospheric temperature in an indoor scene or water temperature in a scene in which the body has been removed from the water)

4) Searching dead bodies
    a) Note any obvious absences of valuables, such as wallet.
    b) Note any indented or pale areas of the body where jewelry may have been worn.
    c) In cases of death excluding homicides and tentative identifications, try to release valuables and money to next of kin at the scene.
    d) Never remove any article of clothing, jewelry, or other item on unidentified remains.
        i) Always obtain receipts for any valuables released at any time to any person.
    e) Have a witness present for any search involving a dead body. An inventory of valuables should be documented in your report.
        i) Do not attempt to describe jewelry, for example, as a diamond ring with a gold band. You are not a jeweler. The item will more correctly be described as a clear stone on a yellow metal band.

5) Moving dead bodies
    a) Do not move body until all photographs, examinations, and measurements have been completed.
    b) Move or lift the body the shortest distance necessary.

    c) Do not contaminate the scene while going to retrieve the body or leaving the scene with the body. Avoid spilling blood onto the scene, if at all possible.

    d) The body should be placed in a clean sheet that is securely wrapped around the decedent and not removed until it arrives at the morgue.

    e) Decedent's hands should be placed in paper bags at the scene prior to the body's being moved.
        i) Bags should be secured in such a way that no mark is left on the decedent's wrist. Use evidence tape, for example, rather than elastic bands.

INDOOR SCENE SEARCHES

1) Start at the body area. Zone the area off and away from the body. Begin examining these zones for evidence. Do not exclude ceiling areas, especially in suspected beating deaths for blood cast-off.

2) Check other rooms away from the house.
    a) Look under bookcases, furniture, etc.
    b) Look in such unlikely places as stoves, voids, canisters, foodstuff, books, etc.

3) Systematically check and note the condition of the following:
    a) Doors
        i) Locked or unlocked?
        ii) Bolted from inside or outside?
        iii) Any marks of forced entry?
        iv) Does doorbell work?
        v) Is there a doorknocker?
    b) Windows
        i) Describe type.
        ii) Locked or unlocked?
        iii) Position of window catch?
    c) Type and position of curtains, drapes, or blinds
        i) Ability to see into the residence?
    d) Other papers and mail
        i) Unopened or recently opened mail
    e) Lighting
        i) Identify which lights were on when the crime was discovered. Can they be seen from the outside?
    f) Smell
        i) Any gas, alcohol, or other odor that is particularly noticeable?
    g) Kitchen area
        i) Food being prepared? What kind (may or may not correspond to decedent's stomach contents or give time-frame indication)?
        ii) How many place settings of utensils, glasses, etc., are present?
        iii) Is ice melted? Food rancid? Liquid stains evaporated?
    h) Heating conditions
        i) What type? Vented or not vented? Stove used to heat area? Thermostat setting?
    i) Fireplace used?
        i) Any residue indicative of efforts to burn evidence?
    j) Contents of ashtrays
        i) Cigarettes, butts, packs, brand, lipstick marks?
    k) Contents of wastebaskets and trashcans. (Be sure to include trash Dumpsters in adjacent areas when apartments or businesses are involved.)

        i) Has anyone been through looking for things?

        ii) Any evidence thrown away?

l) Clocks and watches

        i) Wind-up or electric?

        ii) Are they running?

        iii) Do they show the correct time?

        iv) When did they stop?

        v) What time is the alarm set for?

m) Bath and toilet areas

        i) Are towels, rags, etc., damp or bloodstained?

        ii) Check attempts of suspect to destroy evidence or wash himself.

        iii) Examine medicine cabinets for drugs.

n) General disorder

        i) Evidence of a struggle?

o) Ransacking

        i) To what degree, if any, has the scene been ransacked?

        ii) Was anything stolen?

p) Stairs, passages, entries, and exits to the scene

        i) Check for footprints, debris, and discarded items.

        ii) Attempt to determine the route the suspect may have used to enter and exit the scene.

        iii) Look for hiding places for weapons that the suspect may have concealed quickly.

            (1) Check behind stoves, on top of high furniture, behind books in a bookcase, among bedclothes, under the mattress, etc.

q) Blood

        i) Location

        ii) Degree of coagulation

        iii) Type of stains

OUTDOOR SEARCHES

1) Conduct a detailed search by using a single line of police personnel in a methodical manner.

    a) If necessary, the area should be cleared and divided into grids with twine.

        i) Conduct a systematic search of each grid area.

            (1) Use metal detectors.

            (2) Use sifter (fiberglass screen and water).

            (3) Under ideal conditions, one person should be assigned as a photographer and another participant should be used as recorder to collect evidence while accompanying the searchers.

EVIDENCE AT THE CRIME SCENE

1) The removal and recording of evidence should be restricted to one person. This will preclude:

    a) A long list of persons handling evidence

    b) Several lists of evidence found at crime scene

    c) Eventual court appearances by several persons introducing evidence

2) In the obvious exceptions when more than one investigator is required to record evidence, the chain of custody should be minimized.

3) Points to remember in collecting evidence:

Outdoor scene searches do not usually have the scene boundaries marked by the natural barriers of an indoor scene. Establishing a perimeter in consideration of such evidence as drag and tire marks may be critical to solving a homicide in which the body was found outdoors.

A police helicopter was used to retrieve the body in this case where trace evidence may have been jeopardized if ropes and hooks had been used. Waves created by the helicopter were used to bring the homicide victim's body to shore.

a) Give complete description, date, time, location of recovery, and who recovered it.
b) Give the names of the persons involved in the chain of custody.
c) Specify if a search warrant was used, giving details.
d) When listing evidence, give exact location where it was found and describe the item fully with relationship to incident.

WRAPPING UP THE CRIME SCENE

1) Before leaving, make notes of license tags of vehicles in the area.

2) Canvass the neighborhood.
    a) All interviews should be documented, regardless of the extent of the response.
    b) Obtain names of all persons who reside in each house.
    c) Continue interviews until all persons have been interviewed.
    d) Establish rapport with persons interviewed, leaving your name and phone number, so that they can contact you with additional information.
    e) Reinterview particular neighbors or witnesses, as necessary.

3) Consult with the prosecuting attorney and medical examiner or coroner about releasing the scene.

SEARCH LOCATIONS
(AS SUGGESTED BY THE NAVAL CRIMINAL INVESTIGATIVE SERVICE)

1) Residences and businesses:
    a) Living areas

Behind walls	Inside telephone bases and handles
Behind baseboards and molding	Under number plate of telephones
Inside room dividers	Pay telephone coin return slots
Inside door chimes and door bells	Behind wall phones
Inside stairway posts	Inside clocks
Behind wall outlets and switches	Inside hollow doors (removable top)
In wall and ceiling light fixtures	Inside hollow curtain rods
In bases of lamps	In furniture upholstery
Inside transoms over doorways	Inside hidden drawers in tables
In doorknobs	Under or inside hassocks
Behind picture frames	Inside Bibles (hollow book)
Behind mirrors	In magazines and books
Behind posters	In art kits
In hems of drapes and curtains	In musical instruments and cases
Behind curtains	Inside ironing board covers
Rolled up in window shades	In ironing board legs
Behind acoustical ceiling tiles	In clothespin bags

Above false ceilings

Under carpets

Under throw rugs

Inside electric baseboard heaters

Under false bottom on radiator covers

Inside/behind vacuum cleaner bags

Inside heat and air ducts

Inside chimneys

Inside portable radios/CDs

Inside televisions and stereos

Inside TV tube

Inside TV antennas

In miniature chess boards

In 35mm film canisters

In flashlights

Inside string mops

In and under flower pots

Inside hollowed-out flashlight batteries

Inside shoe polish containers and cases

Inside handle of vacuum cleaners

In bird cages

Under typewriters and covers

Inside letters

Inside hollowed-out pads of paper

Mixed with tobacco

Inside sealed cigarette packages

In dog collars

In pet boxes

In bottom of dog food bags

Behind removable air conditioning registers

b) Attic and basement areas

Around furnaces

In fuel tanks and oil heaters

Inside conduit from fuse boxes

Inside Christmas decorations

In surfboards

Inside hollow legs of outdoor furniture

In attic insulation

Inside tube and barrel of air rifles

Inside abandoned plumbing

In toolboxes

Inside seams and legs of field cots

Inside boxes

c) Bedroom areas

Inside or under mattresses

Inside hidden boxes in mattress frames

Inside bed posts

Inside pillow cases

In false bottom of baby cribs

Inside foot lockers

In jewelry boxes

In false floor of closets

Inside closet clothes rods

Taped to boxes

Inside and under wigs

In hollow canes

In dolls

In clothing

d) Bathroom area

Under bathtubs

Inside toilet paper rolls

Inside razor blade slot disposal

In razor blade dispensers

In shower nozzle heads

Inside shower curtain rods

Behind plumbing inspection doors

Under sinks

Inside toilet tanks

Inside handle of toilet brushes

In clothes hamper

Behind and inside medicine cabinets

In shaving brush handles

In toothpaste tubes

In electric toothbrushes/holders

In hair dryers

In talcum and cold-cream containers

In prescription bottles

Inside sanitary napkins and boxes

In douche containers

e) Kitchen area

In range hoods and filters

In stovepipes

Under burner elements

Behind cabinet kick plates

Under sinks

In sink traps

In garbage disposal

Under lip ring of plastic containers

In toaster crumb trays

In false bottoms on pots and pans

In all canisters and containers

Inside knife handles

Inside rolling pins

In deep-well fryers

In fake beer/soda cans

In fruit containers in refrigerator

In garbage bags

In eggs

In tea bags

In bottom half of double boilers

Inside baked goods

Inside tube of paper towel rolls

f) Outdoor area of building

Inside mailboxes

Under corner mailboxes

In trees (hollowed-out areas)

In rain gutters and downspouts

Under fence post caps

In and under doghouses

Inside animal cages (rabbits, hamsters, etc.)

Under steps

In window boxes

In clothesline pipes

Hanging out of windows

In rice paper

In flash paper

2)   Automobiles

a) Dashboard area

In and over sun visors

In ornamental objects

Inside instrument panels

In fuse boxes

In false radios

In radio speaker grilles

Inside dashboard knobs

In heaters

In and under ashtrays

In vents

In cigarette lighters

In glove compartments

b) Interior

Under brake and gas pedals

Under floorboards

Behind battery boxes

Inside light sockets

In doors

Inside and between seat consoles

Inside and under all seats

In shift knobs

Inside dome lights

Under upholstery

Inside, behind, and under armrests

Taped to rolled-down windows

Under rugs

c) Trunk

Inside trunks

Inside trunk lids

Under false bottoms

Inside spare tire

In spare tire wells

In service station travel kits

In picnic jugs or coolers

Inside flashlights

d) Engine area

In or under insulation under hoods

In air filters

Inside carburetors

Inside hollow batteries

In hollow voltage regulators

In false heater or heater hoses

Inside oil caps

In windshield washer fluid containers

Inside horns

e) Exterior

Taped behind bumpers

Behind license plates

In antenna bases

Under chrome work

Inside bumpers or other type racks

In hubcaps

Under tire valve caps

Under convertible tops

Inside tubing on roof racks

Inside or behind headlights

f) Underside

Behind rocker panels

Inside false dual mufflers

Inside magnetic key cases

Tied to axles

In exhaust pipes

Inside fenders

Attached to frames

Inside gas tanks

g) Miscellaneous

Inside taxicab roof lights

Inside motorcycle handlebar tubing

3)   Body searches

a) Head

In hair and wig

Under false caps on teeth

In ears

Under false teeth

Inside artificial eye

In hearing aid and battery box

In nose

Taped behind ears

Inside mouth

In hearing aid glasses

b) Torso and limbs

Under Band-Aid and bandages

In vagina

Under casts

In rectum

In false limbs

Between cheeks of buttocks

Taped under breasts

Between toes and taped to feet

Under foreskin of penis

c) Underclothing

In bra

In corset

In jock strap

In or under money belt

Pinned to shorts

In swimming trunks

In girdle (male and female)

d) Outer clothing

In or under hair barrettes

In hats

Under lapels of jackets and coats

In or under belt buckles

Behind collar and collar stays

Inside slit or zippered belts

In knot of ties

Under or inside waistbands

In or under tie pins, clasps. or cuff links

Inside fly of trousers

Inside linings of clothing

Inside pockets

Under false buttons

In or behind handkerchiefs

Under cap pins or insignias

Inside pants cuffs

Under patches

Behind ribbons and uniform brass

In socks and shoes

Under insulation in motorcycle helmets

e) Jewelry

Inside or under rings and earrings

Inside neck and wrist lockets

Inside back of watch

Inside identification bracelets

In or under bracelets and charms

f) Handbags and pocket articles

Inside pens

In cigarette lighters

In cigarette packages

In cigarette filters

In tobacco tins and pouches

In stems of pipes

In eyeglass cases

In contact lens cases

Inside lipstick tubes

In compacts

In inhalers

In pill vials

In addressed envelopes

In sticks of gum

In 35mm film canisters

In wallets

Inside lining of change purses

g) Miscellaneous

Inside sanitary napkins or tampons

Inside colostomy bags

In baby diapers

In hollowed-out cane or umbrella handles

Inside hollowed-out crutches

Inside lining of suitcases

In canteens

In Thermos jugs

CHAPTER 2: DEAD BODY EXAMINATION

NOTE: Do not proceed in examining, touching, or moving the body without the express consent of the coroner or medical examiner responsible for certifying the death.

EXAMINATION OF THE BODY FOR PHYSICAL EVIDENCE

1) The time frame used by death investigators for the recovery of evidence from a body is often very inadequate.

2) Investigators usually work all evidence from the outside of a scene toward the inside of a scene, making their way toward the body.
    a) This presents a time dilemma to investigators looking for a possible latent print that may have been left on the victim's remains.
        i) The faster the investigator can work in processing the body, the greater the chances for the death investigator to develop viable physical evidence.
        ii) The more the victim is handled or moved, the greater the chances for physical evidence to be lost, missed, or destroyed.

3) The areas leading to and from the body need to be searched for the location, identification, and collection of potential evidence that may be important to the case.
    a) Death-scene investigators must clear an area to and from and around the victim in an effort to process that body competently and thoroughly.

4) If a search is to be conducted for the possibility of recovering latent fingerprints on the body of the deceased, the following procedure should be used:
    a) Place the remains on top of a new white sheet that has been placed on a backboard.
    b) Wrap the sheet around the body. Do not wrap the sheet tightly. If a second sheet is necessary, use a clean white sheet and lay it on top of the body. Again, do not wrap this sheet tightly around the body.
    c) If the surface skin temperature of the decedent is greater than 80° Fahrenheit (F), the decedent, upon reaching the morgue, should be cooled to approximately 72°F.

FINGERPRINT FORMATION

1) There are three main glands that contribute to the residue necessary for the deposit of fingerprints.
    a) Eccrine glands
        i) These are the only glands located on the fingers, palms of hands, toes, and soles of feet.
        ii) They produce both organic and inorganic residue.
    b) Apocrine glands
        i) These are found on various parts of the body.
        ii) They produce organic residue, which produces bacterial degradation. They are the source for body odor.
    c) Sebaceous glands
        i) These are found on all parts of the body except the fingers, palms, toes, and soles of the feet.

EXAMINATION OF THE BODY AT THE SCENE

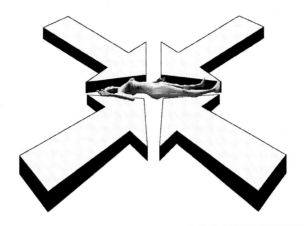

Eyeball area leading to and from area where decedent is. Develop a pathway to use to and from body.

Using an alternate light source (ALS) or other lighting sources, examine pathway for evidence.

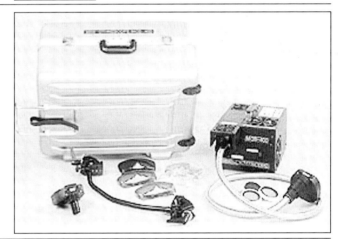

Identify and develop any footprints leading to or away from the body.

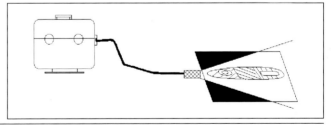

Identify and collect any evidence along the pathway.

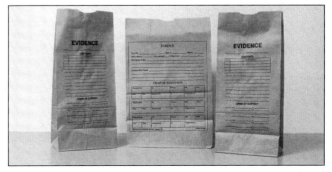

EXAMINATION OF THE BODY AT THE SCENE

 Examine the body. Determine if it may have been moved, undressed, or posed. Examine it for physical evidence.

 Examine, very carefully, those areas that may have been touched by the perpetrator to effect the decedent's observed position or state of dress or undress.

Examining the Body at the Scene

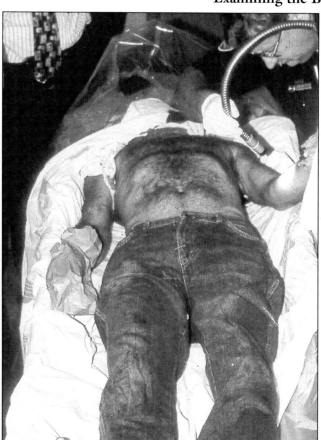

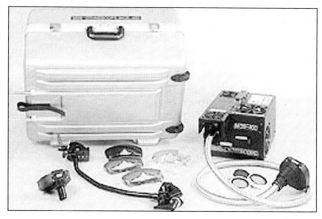

ALS may be able to reveal physical evidence that may go undetected by traditional methods.

Examine the body with various light frequencies, using white light, ultraviolet light, ALS (with various filters for different light emissions).

EXAMINING THE BODY FOR EVIDENCE

If the body has been dragged or carried, carefully examine those areas of the body that the killer would have had to handle in transporting, moving, or killing the victim.

Finger wipes visible on the decedent's skin should be more closely examined for finger or palm ridge detail.

LOCATING FINGERPRINTS ON BODIES

Photograph these potential fingerprint sites before making any effort to use any type of chemical to further enhance the area.

COLLECTING PHYSICAL EVIDENCE FROM THE BODY

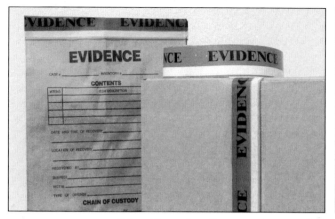 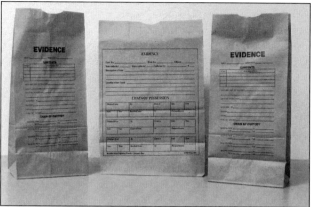

Identify and collect any items of physical evidence that may be lost or
destroyed through the transport of the victim's remains.

ii) They are responsible for producing the fatty or greasy (organic compound) residue creating some fingerprints.

2) Fingerprint residue is also composed of water and alcohol.
   a) The residue from these substances dissipates fairly quickly when left on a surface. In addition, the residue may be absorbed in the victim's skin substrate.
   b) Fatty and greasy residue may last for much longer periods.

3) The appropriate processing method for possibly retrieving the fingerprint residue is dependent, like other fingerprint processing considerations, on the type of surface the print residue was deposited on and the type of chemical, powder, or developer that would be more conducive to the recovery of that print.
   a) For example, processing a suspected print with fingerprint powder and a brush may serve only to destroy or smudge the print because of its moisture content. During the evaporation process, the print becomes somewhat fixed before it diffuses into the preexisting oil.
   b) Like other objects, fingerprints on skin are best developed with brush and powder when the ridge detail of the finger contains residue composed of fatty or greasy substances exuded from the sebaceous glands.

WHERE TO LOOK FOR LATENT PRINTS ON THE BODY

1) The type of incident may indicate the likelihood finding latent prints on the remains.
   a) Various types of homicide and some suicides may involve the potential to place latent prints on the body either on an antemortem, a peri-mortem and/or a post-mortem basis.
      i) Suicides may involve efforts to cover up the true manner of death.

2) Other elements of the crime scene that may indicate the possibly of finding latent fingerprints on the decedent are as follows:
   a) Posing of the decedent
      i) Victims found in a position to elicit some type of effect are likely to have been handled

by the poser. Search for latent prints, including latent prints placed because of some type of contaminant on the ridges of the poser's ridge detail of the gripping surface of his hands or fingers.

(1) Concentrate on areas of the victim's body that would have been necessary to touch to have placed the victim in the observed position.

b) Removal of clothing

i) Any area the perpetrator may have had to touch to remove the victim's clothing should be examined for possible latent prints.

c) Physical confrontation

i) The victim's body should be searched for latent prints in any scene in which it is evident—because of injuries sustained by the victim, the obvious disturbance evident at the scene, or other factors—that the victim and the perpetrator had to be in close physical contact.

d) Playing with the victim's body after death

i) A search for latent prints on the victim's body should be conducted on any scene in which there is indication that the perpetrator played with, had sex with, showed sexual curiosity toward, and/or inflicted postmortem mutilation on the body

e) Areas of injuries that may have been made through the use of fingers

i) Finger impressions may be visible as areas of bruising or scratch marks.

LATENT PRINT EXAMINATION OF SKIN

1) In most cases where latent prints of the murderer were successfully lifted from the victim's skin the prints were detected because of some contaminant present on the hands or fingers of the killer. These contaminants may include, but are not limited to blood, dirt, lipstick, wet paint, and Vaseline.

2) For this reason, any latent print examination should begin with a close, thorough examination of the victim's skin, clothing, and other possible receptacles for deposited prints of the killer.

3) The crime-scene investigator should be able to determine whether the body has been carried or dragged, or whether the cause of death made it necessary for the decedent and the perpetrator to be in close contact with one another.

a) If the body has been dragged or carried, carefully examine those areas of the body that the killer would have to handle in transporting, moving, or killing the victim.

b) Finger wipes visible on the decedent's skin should be more closely examined for finger or palm ridge detail. Photograph these potential fingerprint sites before attempting to use any type of chemical to enhance the area.

4) An ALS or portable laser (viewing through AR goggles with various filters) should also be used to see latent prints that may not be readily visible in room light or daylight but glow brightly when excited with various wavelengths of light.

a) The use of an ALS to distinguish invisible prints or other marks on the victim's skin requires the crime-scene investigator to be skilled in the use of special photographic techniques to capture this image.

5) Identifying latent prints on human skin depends on several factors, including:

a) Contaminants that may affect the ridge detail on the gripping surface of the fingers or on the palms of the hands

b) The particular area of the body touched by the assailant

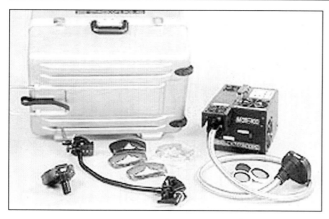

Alternate light source.

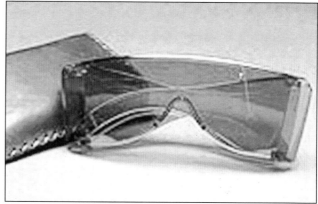

Goggle used with an ALS.

    i) The chemicals in latent prints are the same ones that are naturally deposited on the skin's surface.

    ii) Diffusion of the latent print does not necessarily occur when an oily print is placed on the oily skin's surface of the victim. This process actually takes some time to occur and can be slowed dramatically by lowering the surface temperature of the victim's skin.

        (1) The print can be fixed in place by "superglue fuming" (see p. 23 for more details).

c) The condition of the decedent's skin

    i) The potential for retrieving latent prints is directly related to the body's decomposition status.

    ii) Water or moisture alone will not destroy latent fingerprints on the skin's surface. Some fingerprints are created by fatty or oily substances.

d) Environmental conditions affecting the skin's temperature

    i) The temperature of the decedent's exposed skin will seek the ambient temperature of the environment.

    ii) The latest studies indicate that condensation does not affect the ability to retrieve fingerprints under certain conditions. Fingerprints have been retrieved in experiments where the condensation was allowed to evaporate.

    iii) Current recommendations actually suggest refrigerating the body if the skin temperature is above 80°F for up to 8 hours. The body should then be placed in a room with a temperature of 72°F for 1 hour prior to processing for fingerprints on skin.

        (1) This will solidify the fatty or greasy component of the print.

        (2) It will slow down the diffusion of the print onto the oily substances already present on the victim's skin.

        (3) Moisture from refrigeration may add to the humidity necessary for maximum retrieval potential of the print.

e) Time

    i) The amount of time that has elapsed between the depositing of the print and the examination for its presence.

6) Other problems associated with lifting prints from the decedent's skin

    a) The elasticity of the victim's skin may have temporarily collapsed from the pressure of the perpetrator's fingers in squeezing or pushing on the skin.

i) The latent print may appear as a finger wipe or a smudge. The investigator should carefully search the immediate area for second and third joints of the perpetrator's prints. The gripping surfaces of these areas do not adhere to the skin's surface with the same force as that of the first joint.

    (1) Although these areas aren't entered into Automated Fingerprint Identification Systems (AFIS), they still may be suitable for comparison with a known or suspected suspect.

ii) The skin may be stretched evenly in an effort to visualize detail of the print.

    (1) This can be accomplished by applying a sponge to the back of the lifting medium and maintaining steady pressure for approximately 3 to 4 seconds before releasing, allowing the skin to return to its normal position.

b) Use of a nontransparent medium

i) The use of a nontransparent medium causes the print to be recovered in an inverted position. If a print is to be useful for investigators, the investigator must realize that it is inverted. AFIS submissions and identification will not be successful if the print is incorrectly oriented.

    (1) The print must be converted to a positive print for proper identification by an examiner.

PRELIMINARY STEPS FOR OBTAINING LATENT PRINTS FROM HUMAN SKIN

1) Examine the body and determine the suspected presence of a residual latent print.

2) Consider the possible evaporative conditions created by the body's location and the environmental factors.

3) Consider the rapid diffusion effects the environmental and skin temperature may have on any latent fingerprint residue.

4) Determine the skin temperature of the decedent. Facilitate optimal conditions.

5) Determine what method will be most effective for obtaining the latent print.

CAPTURING LATENT PRINTS ON HUMAN SKIN

1) There are two methods for developing latent friction ridge prints on a body: lift transfer and direct cyanoacrylate (superglue) fuming. It is possible to use both methods (lift transfer, then fuming) on cadavers, although most experts tend to use only one or the other.

Lift-Transfer Method

1) The transfer of the residue from the latent fingerprint is made directly to a lifting medium without any prior development.

2) Temperature plays a critical role in the successful capture of the print.

a) The ideal temperature of both the victim's skin and the ambient environment is 72°F. The ideal temperature of the lifting medium is 90°F. Holding a warm card against the cooler body appears to be the best method for transferring prints.

b) Warm the card or other transfer medium with a portable hair dryer just before lifting.

c) On human skin involving live victims, this manner of processing was successful for up to 1 hour after the print was deposited.

3) Magnetic powder may be used after an initial examination of the possible recovery site is made with an ALS.
    a) If the skin surface is in the optimal range of temperature (70–72°F), magnetic powder may be directly applied to the area.
        i) Photograph developed print.
            (1) Shoot one photo with a ruler present and a second one with a scale in the photo with the print. An American Board of Forensic Odontology (ABFO) scale should be used.
        ii) Use a feather brush to remove excess powder from the print, which enhances it.

4) The direct lift is accomplished by placing a nontransparent medium against the skin.
    a) Heat the back of the lifting card with a portable hair dryer.
    b) Apply the card to the skin and hold it for 15 to 20 seconds.
    c) After removing it from the skin, allow the lifting card to air-dry for approximately 10 to 15 minutes to allow the card to lose heat and eventually assume the temperature of the room. Any moisture on the card will evaporate.
    d) The card may then be superglued for approximately 10 to 20 minutes in a "superglue chamber" fashioned from a plastic toolbox or fishing box.
    e) After removing from the card from the superglue chamber, lightly brush magnetic powder against the lift.
    f) Investigators sometimes ignore the superglue process and instead place magnetic powder on the card after the lift is pulled away from the skin and air-dried for 10 to 15 minutes.

5) Nontransparent lifting mediums include the following:
    a) Fixed photo paper (Kodakrome II) cut into 5 x -inch sheets
    b) Kromekote cards, cut into 5 x 7-inch cards.
    c) Cash register tape
    d) Plain white bond paper
    e) Iodine-silver plate technique

6) Types of transparent lifting mediums include the following:
    a) Laminated glass (3 x 5 inches).
    b) Ziploc freezer bags (pint size).
    c) Saran Wrap
    d) Clear plastic
    e) Exposed negative film (70mm)

7) The investigator and any other people who prepare these materials should be very careful that they do not add their own prints to them.

Cyanoacrylate (Superglue) Fuming

1) Superglue fuming is used only on dead victims.

2) Proper fuming works because the ingredients in cyanoacrylate adheres to the salts and lipids of the residual print on the skin surface of the decedent.

3) The best environment for the recovery of fingerprints from the body appears to be one with 80 percent humidity. In dry environments, the fuming chamber's humidity may be adjusted for more humidity by adding a container with warm water inside the fuming chamber. The best temperature is 80°F.

      a) In studies, the use of superglue fuming in temperatures below 68°F was highly unsuccessful.

4) For fuming, assemble an airtight plastic tent over the body and use heat acceleration (coffee cup warmers) accompanied by a small, battery-powered fan to distribute the fumes evenly. The smaller the chamber, the faster the reaction time.

      a) The fan should be battery powered because sparks from a 110-volt electric fan motor is a fire hazard in a confined fuming chamber.

5) Test strips of plastic or aluminum bearing a "test" latent print should always be fumed with the body. If the test impression has developed, examine the body. One of two conditions will exist:

      a) A fully developed print will be visible or a partial print will appear, requiring further processing with fingerprint powder.

         i) If the print needs further processing, dust with a contrasting color powder.

            (1) Using a feather duster with fluorescent powder is sometimes successful, but black magnetic powder is used more often. Black magnetic powder usually "paints" the skin less, doesn't require a laser or an ALS, and is easier to photograph.

6) In his book, *Recovery of Latent Fingerprint Evidence from Human Skin: Causation, Isolation, and Processing Techniques*, William C. Sampson recommends fuming the body for 8 to 10 hours before processing with magnetic powder and brush.

CONCLUSION

In the real world of homicide investigation, it is often considered impractical to spend an exorbitant amount of time processing bodies for latent print development. Medical examiners, coroners, police detectives, and other death investigators are often not very patient when awaiting the opportunity to perform their function at a homicide scene.

It would be ideal to be able to spend 8 hours with one body to obtain a possible print. But because of caseloads, schedules, and a very low success rate, this type of processing is very often considered impractical. Frankly, since the 1970s the cases in which a print has been recovered have numbered only a couple of dozen, and prints ultimately linked to the bad guy have any been more remote. Convincing a medical examiner or coroner to allow a body to decompose at the scene while an evidence technician attempts to stain or chemically process a body because there is the remote possibility of retrieving a print from the remains takes a trusting relationship. Throughout their entire careers, most practitioners will never experience a case in which a latent print is successfully lifted from a dead body.

CHAPTER 3: CRIME-SCENE SEARCHES

Various methods of crime-scene searches are employed in an effort to be as productive as possible based on the number of staff available or the type of scene involved. The specific search methods are sector or zone, ever-widening circle, straight line, strip, and grid.

SECTOR OR ZONE SEARCH

1) This method is used in homicide, rape, drug searches, and bomb cases where it is necessary to search a small area or a room. It can be done by one person but is more effective if after one person searches, a second person completes a separate search of the same area.

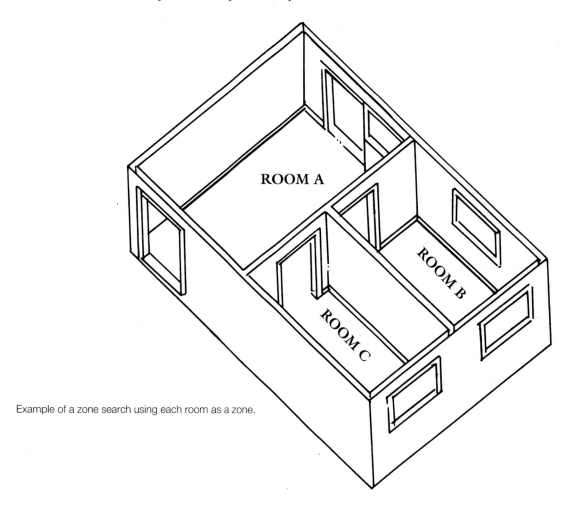

Example of a zone search using each room as a zone.

EVER-WIDENING-CIRCLE SEARCH

1) This involves a searcher beginning at the center of an area, usually dictated by the subject or object involved, and continuing in ever-widening circles away from the object until the entire area is covered.

2) It is usually implemented when only one person is available for the search.

CIRCLE SEARCH

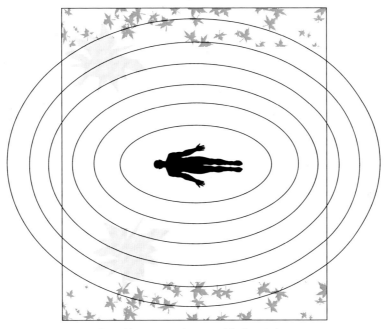

Searching a scene in ever-widening circles.

STRAIGHT-LINE SEARCH

1) It is usually employed in large, outdoor scenes.

2) It is useful for body-dump cases and mass disasters.

3) It involves a large number of people standing side by side and traveling across the scene in a straight line. Each searcher is responsible for his area.

STRIP SEARCH

1) This is used when only a limited number of people are available for a fairly large area.

Example of a strip-search pattern.

GRID SEARCH

1) It is used in mass disasters and cases involving large areas.

2) Divide the area into grid and search each grid section. Conduct a second search in a perpendicular pattern to the first search.

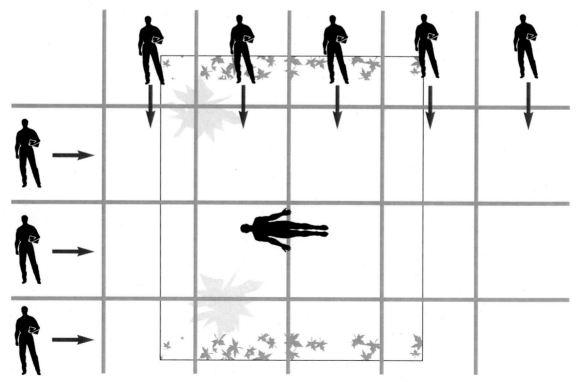

Example of a grid-search pattern.

CHAPTER 4: CRIME-SCENE DRAWINGS

CONSIDERATIONS

1) Depictions of death scenes can be referred to as sketches, diagrams, or drawings.

2) A drawing is used to augment those areas in which a photograph is lacking. Specifically, a drawing is used to depict the locations of items to other items and/or items to scenes without showing all of the details present in a photograph.

3) A drawing should assist in presenting and clarifying investigative data.

4) The drawing can be used for three purposes:
   a) To question persons in an ongoing investigation
   b) To supplement, clarify, and understand the prepared report of the investigation
   c) To present the information to a court

LEGAL ASPECTS

1) To be admissible, the drawing must be a part of some qualified person's testimony.

2) The witness may tender the drawing to the court in connection with his testimony. If the judge thinks the drawing would be helpful in making the testimony clear, then the drawing is admitted.

3) The drawing may have been made by the witness or somewone who prepared it under the supervision of the testifying witness.

PREPARING THE DRAWING

1) A rough sketch and finished sketch should be prepared for each drawing.
   a) The investigator at the scene draws the rough sketch. It does not need to be drawn to scale, but the correct measurements (including accurate distances, dimensions, and relative proportions) are included in the drawing.
   b) The finished drawing is completed under office conditions. The sketch is drawn to scale based on the measurements indicated in the rough sketch.

MEASURING METHODS

1) Coordinate method
   a) An object is measured from two fixed points or from a baseline drawn between two fixed points. The baseline may also be a wall. The measurements of a given object are then taken from left to right along the baseline to a point at right angles to the object being measured.
   b) This method is common for indoor scenes.

2) Triangulation method
   a) Choose two or more widely separated reference points. Then measure the object from a straight line from each reference point.
   b) This method is especially useful for outdoor scenes.

COORDINATION MEASUREMENT TECHNIQUE

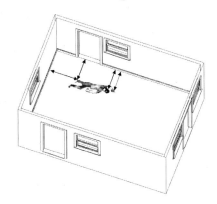

TRIANGULATION MEASUREMENT TECHNIQUE

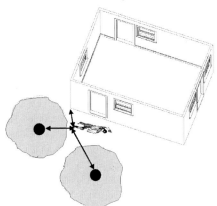

INFORMATION INCLUDED IN ALL DRAWINGS

1) The investigator's full name
2) The date, time, crime classification, and case number
3) The full name of any person assisting in taking measurements
4) Address of the crime scene, its position in a building, landmarks, and compass direction
5) The scale of the drawing if a scale has been used or a disclaimer if no scale was used
6) The major items of physical evidence and the measurements involving these items
7) A legend or key to the symbols (numbers) used

TYPES OF DRAWINGS

1) Floor plan or bird's-eye view
    a) Most common of all drawings

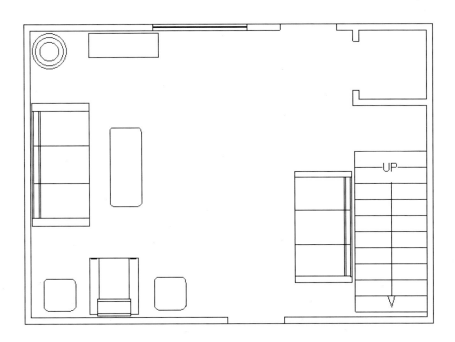

An example of a bird's-eye view crime-scene drawing.

2) Exploded view
    a) Similar to the floor plan except the walls and ceiling have been laid out flat
    b) Especially useful when objects of interest are on wall surfaces as well as the floor
    c) Used when depicting blood spatter, gunshot holes, fingerprint locations, etc.

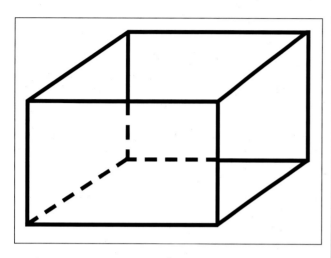

1

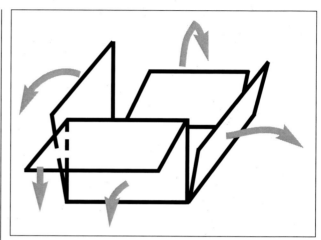

2

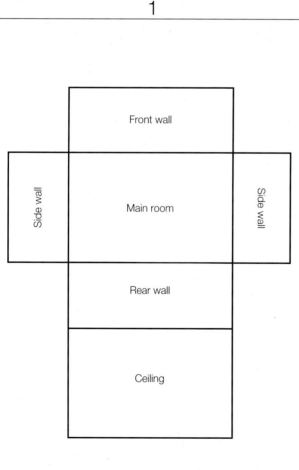

3

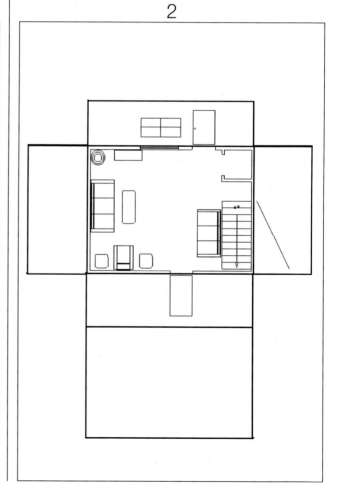

4

Exploded-view drawing.

3) Three-dimensional drawings
    a) Used in the following ways:
        i) To supplement photographs of the scene
        ii) To provide a reference or orientation for clarifying testimony supplied by witnesses
        iii) To demonstrate the relative positions of critical evidence in a three-dimensional setting
    b) Examples include bullet holes, shell casings, recovered projectiles, blood spatter projections, etc.

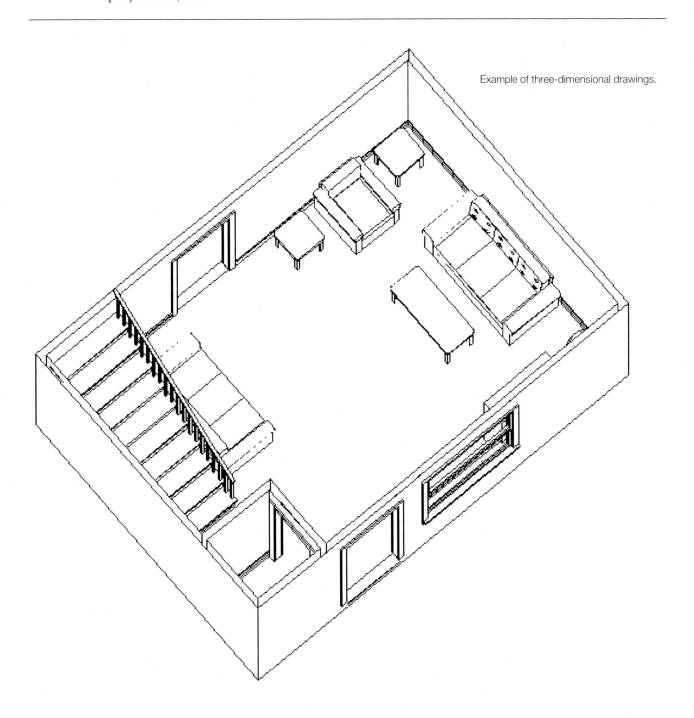

Example of three-dimensional drawings.

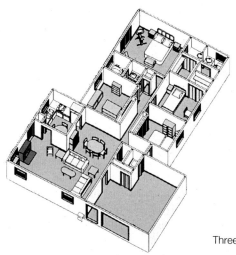

Three-dimensional crime scene from a different perspective.

Camera view from within three-dimensional drawing.

Additional camera view from crime-scene bedroom.

Reenactment of shooting from crime-scene drawing.

TOTAL STATION

1) Considerations:
    a) Used on crime scenes and traffic crash scenes involving a fairly expansive area.
    b) The legitimate use of this tool is for surveying. It allows the quick processing of a large area, which may contain many physical features as well as a large amount of evidence.

2) Types of scenes that may benefit from the quick processing capabilities of a total station:
    a) Outdoor scenes involving a vast area with a large amount of evidence
    b) Traffic crashes, hit-and-run accidents, and multiple-vehicle crashes

3) How it works:
    a) A total station sends (electronic transit) and receives an electronic signal (electronic distance-measuring device, or EDM).
        i) With this device, angles and distances from the instrument to points to be surveyed can be measured. With the aid of trigonometry, the angles and distances can be used to calculate the actual positions of surveyed points in absolute terms.
    b) The other part of a total station, the EDM, measures the distance from the instrument to its target.

     i) The EDM sends out an infrared beam, which is reflected back to the unit, and the unit uses timing measurements to calculate the distance traveled by the beam.

c) The total station also includes a simple calculator to figure the locations of points sighted. The calculator can perform the trigonometric functions needed, starting with the angles and distance, to calculate the location of any point sighted.

d) Total stations used for crime scenes also include data recorders. The raw data (angles and distances) and/or the coordinates of points sighted are recorded, along with some additional information (usually codes to aid in relating the coordinates to the points surveyed).

     i) The data recorded can be directly downloaded to a computer at a later time.

     ii) Using a data recorder further reduces the potential for error and eliminates the need for a person to record the data in the field.

e) The total station is mounted on a tripod and leveled before use. Meanwhile the prism is mounted on a pole of known height.

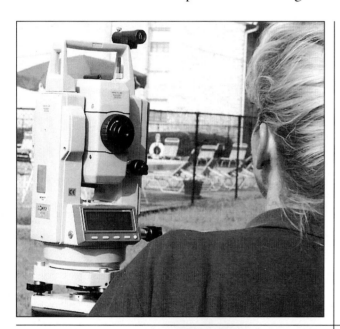

A total station–survey type tool was used to show the relationship of all of the apartment buildings to one another at this homicide scene. Using a total-station susrvey allows processing at the scene to be completed fairly quickly in spite of the large area involved.

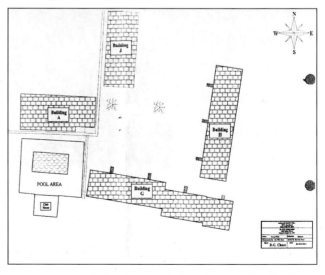

Drawing courtesy of Officer D. Chase, Jacksonville, Florida, Sheriff's Office.

CHAPTER 5: PHOTOGRAPHING A DEATH SCENE

BASICS

1) Take photographs to assist in explaining what happened, as well as how and when it may have happened.

2) The camera should be held at eye level on every shot showing the relationship of an object to the scene.

EXTERIOR SHOTS

1) An overall view of the area to show the remoteness of area if applicable to the type of crime or to the facilitating of the particular crime (consider aerial photography)

2) The relationship of the building or vehicle to other buildings, streets, or landmarks

3) The address of involved residence or vehicle identification if a vehicle is involved

4) Tire impressions

5) Foot or shoe impressions

6) Discarded cigarettes or cigarette packs

7) Discarded cans or cups

8) Broken branches or disturbed shrubbery

9) Drag marks

10) Any articles left behind

11) Any weapon(s)

12) Any other evidence that might relate to the death
    a) Shell casings
    b) Expended projectiles
    c) Live rounds
    d) Articles of clothing

13) Blood spatter relating to movement or activity of the victim or suspect

INTERIOR SHOTS (INCLUDING VEHICLES)

1) The room or area in which the decedent was found

2) The adjoining rooms or areas associated with the death. Even if they do not appear to be related to the incident, subsequent investion or analysis may prove that these areas were important in understanding the sequence of events and/or may corroborate or dispute developing information.

3) Evidence of a struggle
    a) Torn or bloody clothing
    b) Overturned furniture
    c) Rifled drawers, jewelry boxes, purses, wallets, safes, desks, and other areas where valuables may have been contained (photograph these items even if they appear undisturbed)
    d) Broken windows or glass articles
    e) Bloodstains
    f) Other objects strewn about or that appear not to be in their usual positions
        i) Telephone handsets off the receivers
        ii) Cut telephone lines

4) Photograph any items that may indicate a disruption in the victim's activities at the time of death.
    a) Preparation of a meal
    b) Television and light status
    c) Number and type of eating utensils (e.g., glasses, coffee cups, plates)
    d) Liquor bottles, wine bottles, or beer cans (empty or filled) that may be associated with the scene or activities from the scene

5) Photograph areas that indicate that an object may have been taken or is missing (e.g., dust on top of the television that indicates the possible absence of a VCR).

6) Status of locks on windows and doors
    a) Condition of chain hasp on door
    b) Signs of break-in

7) Any unusual signs
    a) Door ajar
    b) Windows open
    c) Lights on during the daytime
    d) Notes, letters, insurance policies, or money left in open areas

8) Trace evidence
    a) Blood stains and spatter
    b) Foot or shoe prints
    c) Hair or fibers
    d) Fingerprint areas
    e) Tool marks

BODY SHOTS

1) Take the photographs as an observer would view the body. The camera should be held at eye level, and the body and scene relationship photographed as an observer would normally view the scene.

2) Photograph the body in relation to the room or vehicle from north, east, south, and west.

3) Photograph the body in relation to certain features or evidence in the room (e.g., possible murder weapon, prescription vials, broken glass).

4) Photograph a close-up of the wound or other areas of injury.

5) Photograph blood spatter on the clothing of decedent.
6) Photograph any areas of bloodletting around or adjacent to the decedent.

7) Photograph any unusual signs of activities involving the decedent's body.
    a) Pockets turned inside out
    b) Unusual placement of possible weapons on, in, or near the body
    c) Insect activity
    d) Animal sctivity

8) Photograph decedent's hands and feet.

9) Photograph any indication of possible drug abuse.

10) Photograph the area under the body once the body has been moved.

11) Photograph any trace evidence observed on the body.

SPECIALIZED PHOTOGRAPHS

1) Check the particular death investigation chapters for the specialized photographs that will be pertinent to each particular type of case.

DIGITAL PHOTOGRAPHY

1) The admissibility of digital photographs in court:
    a) Just as with regular photographs developed from film, digital photographs are subject to the same requirements. Unless the photograph is admitted by the stipulation of both parties, the principal requirements to admit a photograph (digital or film based) into evidence are relevance and authentication.
    b) The party attempting to admit the photograph into evidence must be prepared to offer testimony that the photograph is an accurate representation of the scene. This usually means that someone must testify that the photograph accurately portrays the scene as viewed by that witness.
    c) The major criticism of digital photography is that it may be more easily altered than film-based photographs.

2) Federal court considerations:
    a) Federal Rules of Evidence, Article X (Contents of Writings, Recordings, and Photographs), Rule 101(1) defines writings and recordings to include magnetic, mechanical, or electronic recordings.
        i) Rule 101(3) states that if data are stored in a computer or similar device, any printout or other output readable by sight, shown to reflect the data accurately, is an "original."
        ii) Rule 101(4) states that a duplicate is a counterpart produced by the same impression as the original . . . by mechanical or electronic re-recording . . . or by other equivalent techniques that accurately reproduce the original.
        iii) Rule 103 (admissibility of duplicates) states that a duplicate is admissible to the same extent as an original unless:
            (1) A genuine question is raised as to the authenticity of the original or
            (2) In the circumstances it would be unfair to admit the duplicate in lieu of the original.

3) State court considerations:
   a) Most states have laws that apply to digital evidence.

4) Local legal considerations:
   a) Always check with your legal representative before instituting any new procedure involving the collection of evidence, the processing of a crime scene, or investigation protocol.

5) Guidelines for ensuring that your digital photographs are admissible:
   a) All agencies should develop department policy on the use of digital imaging.
      i) This policy should detail:
         (1) When digital imaging is used
         (2) Chain of custody
         (3) Image security
         (4) Image enhancement
         (5) Release and availability of digital images
      ii) The agency should preserve the original digital image. This should be done by saving and retaining the image to a hard drive or some other recording or imaging file.
   b) Digital images should be preserved in their original file formats.
      i) Attempting to save the file in some other format may result in some change of the image as a result of the compression process.
   c) If images are stored on a computer workstation or server to which several individuals would have access to them, make the files read-only for all but your evidence or photo lab staff.
      i) For example, detectives could view any image files, but they could not delete or overwrite those files.
   d) If an image is to be analyzed or enhanced, the new image files created should be saved as new file names. *The original file must not be replaced (overwritten) with a new file.*

CHAPTER 6: VIDEOTAPING A DEATH SCENE

CONSIDERATIONS

1) When you are on call, check that all gear is in the kits and working properly.

2) Camera techniques
   a) Use videotape to assist in explaining what happened, as well as how and when it may have happened.
   b) Is additional lighting necessary at the scene?
   c) Don't pan the camera from side to side, and up and down. Use one clean sweep, instead.
   d) Always include an exterior or a general view of the subject location.
   e) When covering a long, narrow section of a scene (e.g., road, corridor, railroad track), consider doing a slow zoom from a tripod rather than filming as you walk along the area.
   f) In confined spaces (e.g., toilets, bathrooms) use a high camera angle from a corner to give maximum coverage of the area.
   g) Use a tripod when necessary.
   h) A much more professional product can be produced with a well-planned video. In contrast to still photography, taking more shots is not necessarily better when it comes to videotaping a scene. Unnecessarily repeating or prolonging shots will only bore or confuse, and won't enhance the evidential value of the video.
   i) The camera should be held at eye level on every shot showing the relationship of an object to the scene.
   j) Do not narrate the scene.
   k) Warn all individuals present that the scene is being filmed. Personnel should leave the scene during filming and refrain from conversation in the area of the filming. Disable the sound mechanism of the camera, if possible.
   l) Begin the filming at the perimeter of the scene and work toward the decedent.
   m) The entire scene should be shot initially without any scales or references being placed in the video viewing ara. After shooting the scene, scales and markers can be used for visual-aid purposes.
   n) Give a location perspective to small items on the scene before zooming in for a close-up shot.
      i) Small items should be initially shot without benefit of a scale. The item should be filmed again with a scale present.

3) Legal considerations of videotaping of a scene
   a) A videotaped scene must pass two tests to be admitted into evidence:
      i) It must depict the unaltered scene.
      ii) It must have been maintained in its original condition without any erasures or editing.

4) At the scene
   a) Check with patrol or scene supervisor. Obtain a good and accurate concept of the scene and its history. Information may include the following:
      i) How did the scene/crime unfold?
      ii) What are the scene's boundaries?
      iii) Where is the evidence? Consider the following:
         (1) Shoe impressions
         (2) Tire tracks

　　　(3) Blood
　　　(4) Fibers
　　　(5) Fingerprints
　　　(6) Clothing
　　　(7) Bedding
　　　(8) Impacted vehicles/aircraft
　　　(9) Debris
　　　(10) Any other object with potential evidential value
　iv) Determine the route that will be used when going in to and out of the scene.
　v) Make written notes in an official notebook:
　　　(1) Time and date of arrival
　　　(2) Location details
　　　(3) Victim details (name, etc.)
　　　(4) Names of other team members
　　　(5) Case synopsis

EXTERIOR SHOTS

1) An overall view of the area to show the remoteness of area if applicable to the type of crime or to the facilitating of the particular crime

2) Relationship of building or vehicle to other buildings, streets, or landmarks

3) Address of involved residence or vehicle identification, if vehicle is involved

4) Shoot any evidence discerned at the scene, including but not limited to:
　　a) Tire impressions
　　b) Foot or shoe impressions
　　c) Discarded cigarettes or cigarette packs
　　d) Discarded cans or cups
　　e) Broken branches or disturbed shrubbery
　　f) Drag marks
　　g) Any articles left behind
　　h) Any weapon(s)
　　i) Any other evidence relating to the death
　　　　i) Shell casings
　　　　ii) Expended projectiles
　　　　iii) Live rounds
　　j) Articles of clothing
　　k) Blood spatter relating to movement or activity of the victim or suspect

INTERIOR SHOTS

1) The room or area in which the decedent was found

2) The adjoining rooms or areas associated with the death (even if negative findings)

3) Evidence of a struggle
　　a) Torn or bloody clothing
　　b) Overturned furniture

    c) Rifled drawers, jewelry boxes, purses, wallets, safes, desks, and other areas where valuables may have been contained. (Photograph these items even if they appear undisturbed.)
    d) Broken windows or glass articles
    e) Bloodstains
    f) Other objects strewn about or that appear not to be in their usual positions
        i) Telephone handsets off the receivers
        ii) Cut telephone lines
    g) Drag marks

4) Film any items that may indicate a disruption in the victim's activities at the time of death.
    a) Preparation of a meal
    b) Television or lamps/lights status
    c) Number and type of eating utensils (e.g., glasses, coffee cups, plates)
    d) Liquor bottles, wine bottles, or beer cans (empty or filled) that may be associated with the scene or the activities from the scene

5) Film areas that may show that an object has been taken or is missing (e.g., dust on top of the television that indicates the possible absence of a VCR).

6) Status of locks on windows and doors
    a) Condition of chain hasp on door
    b) Signs of break-in

7) Unusual signs
    a) Door ajar
    b) Window open
    c) Light on during the daytime
    d) Notes, letters, insurance policies, or money left in open areas

8) Trace evidence
    a) Bloodstains and spatter
    b) Foot or shoe prints
    c) Hair or fibers
    d) Fingerprint areas
    e) Tool marks

9) Weapon(s)

10) Any other evidence relating to death
    a) Shell casings, projectiles, or live rounds
    b) Articles of clothing

VEHICLE SHOTS

1) Film in much the same way as interior shots.

2) Shoot a vehicle in relation to other vehicles, buildings, intersections, or landmarks.

3) Shoot any significant tire impression, footprints, or drag marks located outside the vehicle.

4) Film any significant roadway conditions or indications of the vehicle's action prior to coming to a stop.

5) Shoot vehicle from all four sides.
    a) Include registration plate.
    b) Include auto tag.

6) Film the entire interior of the vehicle.

7) Film the interior of the trunk.

8) Film any loose item.

9) Film any trace evidence.

10) Film any internal or external vehicle damage.

11) Film any other item or area that is unusual or may be significant.

BODY SHOTS

1) Take the photographs as an observer would view the body. The camera should be held at eye level, and the body and scene relationship photographed as an observer would normally view the scene.

2) Film the body in relation to the room from all four sides.

3) Film the body in relation to certain features or evidence in the room (e.g., possible murder weapon, prescription vials, broken glass).

4) Film a close-up of the wound and/or other areas of injury.

5) Film blood spatter on the clothing of decedent.

6) Film any areas of bloodletting around or adjacent to the decedent.

7) Film any unusual signs of activities involving the decedent's body.
    a) Pockets turned inside out
    b) Unusual placement of possible weapons on, in, or near the body
    c) Insect activity
    d) Animal activity

8) Film decedent's hands and feet.

9) Film any indication of possible drug abuse.

10) Film the area under the body once the body has been moved.

11) Film any trace evidence observed on the body.

CHAPTER 7: EVIDENCE COLLECTION

	Metal Paint Can	Paper Bag	Glass Vial	Paper Envelope	Cardboard Box	Metal Box	Plastic Bag
Arson material	p. 57						
Blood (air-dried)		p. 48		p. 48			
47X							
Blood (scraping)				p. 48			
Bones					p. 51		
Bullet				p. 59	p. 59		
Bullet casing				p. 60	p. 60		
Charred documents		Hand-deliver to lab					
Cigarette butt				p.52			
Clothing (air-dried)		p. 53					
Clothing (fire-related)	p. 53						
Condom		p. 52		p. 52			
Controlled substances							p. 64
Fabric (air-dried)		p. 54		p. 54			
Fibers				p. 53			
Fingernail scrapings				p. 51			
Flammable material			p. 58				
Fingerprint cards				X			
Firearm					p. 59		
Glass (large fragments)					p. 55		
Gunshot residue					p. 61		p. 61
Hair				p. 51			
Handgun		p. 59			p. 59		

	Metal Paint Can	Paper Bag	Glass Vial	Paper Envelope	Cardboard Box	Metal Box	Plastic Bag
Jewelry							X
Latent prints					p. 67		
Money							X
Narcotics							p. 64
Paint (chips)						p. 57	
Plant material							p. 74
Prescriptive medication							p. 64
Questioned documents							p. 66
Rifle		p. 59			p. 59		
Rock		X			X		
Rope		p. 54					
Saliva swabs (air-dried)				p. 50			
Semen (air-dried)		p. 50		p. 50			
Shoes					p. 54		
Shoe cast					p. 74		
Shotgun		p. 59			p. 59		
Shotgun ammunition					p. 60		
Shotgun wadding				p. 60			
Soil		X			X		
Tire treads					X		
Tool marks		p. 63			p. 63		

EVIDENCE-COLLECTION GUIDELINES

This chapter provides general guidelines for collecting various types of evidence. Your agency's policies may vary. Please check with the crime laboratory used by your agency if there are any questions or considerations involving any particular evidence.

The following items represent some of the evidence that may be encountered in a death investigation. Some features, or the investigative significance of the items, are submitted for consideration. This is in no way a comprehensive listing.

MAJOR CONCERNS OF FORENSIC EXAMINATION, COLLECTION, AND PROCESSING OF EVIDENCE ASSOCIATED WITH THE CRIME SCENE

1) Trace evidence
   a) Be careful at crime scenes that you do not destroy any trace evidence that you may not be able to see.

2) Contamination
   a) The Locard principle of the transfer theory of evidence (in 1892 criminologist Edmond Locard theorized that every contact leaves its trace) may also result in inadvertent cross-contamination of the scene by the examiner or other participants in the crime scene processing.

3) Cross-examination
   a) At some point in the crime-scene technician's career, he may be required to get on the witness stand and give testimony as to why one chemical may have been used instead of another and why the evidence may have been worked in a certain sequence.
      i) For example, a bloody knife—should the technician develop the blood on the knife or superglue the knife for prints? Keep in mind that superglue will destroy the blood evidence. Being able to develop a sequential effort that ensures the full processing capabilities of the evidence is critical to a death investigation.
      ii) When you are considering blood evidence identification versus fingerprint identification, your decision is based on the more exclusive ability of that evidence to make a positive identification. Fingerprint evidence gets priority because it is mutually exclusive. Although DNA evidence is making incredible strides and in some cases DNA experts have testified that in terms of probability DNA evidence is *virtually* mutually exclusive, on a case-to-case, evidence-to-evidence basis, the chances of having fingerprint evidence identify one person, and only one person, is much greater.

BLOODSTAINS

1) Investigative considerations
   a) Reconstructing the event by blood-spatter interpretation (bloodstain analysis)
   b) Maybe establishing the distance of objects or persons at critical moments
   c) Maybe indicating the particular weapon involved due to blood transfer
   d) Maybe identifying the suspect of the crime

2) Blood that is in liquid pools should be picked up on a gauze pad or other clean, sterile cotton cloth and allowed to air-dry thoroughly at room temperature. It should be refrigerated or frozen as soon as possible and brought to the laboratory as quickly as possible. Delays beyond 48 hours may make the samples useless.
   a) If close to the laboratory, deliver the stained object immediately.
   b) If unable to deliver to the laboratory or if the object must be mailed, allow the stain to air-dry completely before packaging.

c) Do not heat stained material or place it in bright sunlight to dry. Hang clothing and similar articles in a room with adequate ventilation.

d) If not completely dry, label and roll in paper or place in a brown paper bag or box and seal and label the container. Place only one item in each container. Do not use plastic containers.

DRIED BLOODSTAINS

1) Investigative considerations
    a) Human versus nonhuman
    b) Links to a particular individual
    c) Possible development of drug identification
    d) Race characteristics
    e) Reconstruction of the event by blood-spatter interpretation (bloodstain analysis)
    f) Possible establishment of distance of objects or persons at critical moments
    g) Possible indication of particular weapon involved due to blood transfer
    h) Possible identification of the crime suspect

2) Collection considerations
    a) On clothing: if possible, wrap the item in clean paper, place the article in a brown paper bag or box, and seal and label container. Do not attempt to remove stains from the cloth.
    b) On small solid objects: send the whole stained item to the laboratory after labeling and packaging it.
    c) On large solid objects: cover the stained area with clean paper and seal the edges down with tape to prevent loss or contamination.
        i) If impractical to deliver the whole object to the laboratory, scrape the stain onto a clean piece of paper, which can be folded and placed in an envelope. Do not scrape directly into evidence envelope.
        ii) Scrape blood from objects using a freshly washed and dried knife or similar tool.
        iii) Wash and dry the tool before each stain is scraped off.
        iv) Seal and mark the envelope.
    d) Do not mix dried stains. Place each stain in a separate envelope.
    e) Never attempt to wipe dried stains from an object using a moistened cloth or paper.

STANDARD BLOOD SPECIMENS

1) Investigative considerations
    a) These may indicate if a crime has been committed (e.g., poisoning, driving under the influence)
    b) These may indicate drug type (including alcohol) and specific levels that are present
    c) These may be typed to a certain level and used for comparison with a suspect sample for identification purposes, which may be used in placing a subject at the scene of a particular crime.
    d) These may be used to determine paternity.
    e) These may refute witness assertion that the subject committed a particular crime

AUTOPSY BLOOD SAMPLES

1)   Collection considerations
     a) Request pathologist to obtain the sample directly from the heart into a yellow-
        or purple-stopper vacutainer (some labs request both). Test tubes with gray, purple,
        and yellow stoppers contain an anticoagulant that prevents the sample from clotting.
        It preserves the blood. A red stopper test tube does not contain an anticoagulant.
     b) In rare cases when no liquid blood is available, ask the pathologist to collect a section
        of liver, bone, or deep muscle tissue and freeze it for typing. In such cases, proceed
        also with collection of a secondary standard as described below.

BLOOD SAMPLES FROM LIVE INDIVIDUALS

1)   Collection considerations
     a) For typing purposes have sample drawn into yellow- and purple-stopper vacutainers.
        Note that these are distinguished from the tubes, which have gray stoppers.
     b) If the victim requires a transfusion, try to obtain or begin necessary procedures to
        obtain the pretransfusion sample collected by the hospital.
          i) These samples are not retained for long periods by the hospital, so it is
             important to act promptly.
          ii) Also, make sure that some bloodstained garment worn by the individual has
             been air-dried and frozen to serve as a secondary standard.

     c) In an effort to prevent cross-contamination (or the appearance that cross-
        contamination may have occurred), never transport the live rape victim and the
        suspect of the crime in the same police or other official vehicle. Likewise, prevent the
        possibility of cross-contamination between victim and suspect by considering other
        common areas to avoid (e.g., the interview room) until such time as the collection of
        personal evidence has occurred.

2)   Handling and storage of physiological fluid evidence
     a) You have an obligation under *People vs. Nation and Hitch* to make a "reasonable and
        good faith effort" to preserve perishable evidence.
     b) Stains and controls
          i) Air-dry.
          ii) Package in paper.
          iii) Freeze.
     c) Consider special handling on nonabsorbent items (e.g., metal or plastic). Any
        condensation from thawing could disturb or destroy such evidence. Such items should
        be kept at room temperature and submitted to the lab as soon as possible.

LIQUIDS (STANDARDS)

Blood

1)   Collection considerations
     a) Refrigerate, do not freeze standards collected in yellow-stopper (ACD) vacutainers.
     b) Submit to the lab as soon as possible.

Saliva

1)   Investigative considerations

a) Serology test to establish consistency or inconsistency with that of a known suspect
b) DNA typing

2) Collection considerations
    a) Collect on sterile gauze pads or swabs.
    b) Air-dry.
    c) Place in paper envelope; do not use plastic containers.

Seminal Stains/Semen

1) Investigative considerations
    a) Serology test to establish consistency or inconsistency of suspect
    b) DNA typing
    c) Element of rape

2) Collection consideration
    a) Seminal stains are often, but not always, found on clothing, blankets, sheets.
    b) Allow any stains to air-dry, wrap them in paper, and package evidence in paper bags. Do not use plastic bags.
    c) For sex offense cases a physician should always examine the victim.
    d) Use a sexual assault evidence collection kit to collect evidence from the victim. It is very important that the instructions on the kit be followed with care to gain the greatest benefit from the collected evidence.
    e) In an effort to prevent cross-contamination (or the appearance that cross-contamination may have occurred), never transport the live rape victim and the suspect of the rape in the same police or other official vehicle. Likewise, prevent the possibility of cross-contamination between victim and suspect by considering other common areas (e.g., the interview room) to avoid until such time as the collection of personal evidence has occurred.
    f) Label all garments (e.g., undershorts, panties, or other exhibits) and package each separately.
    g) If damp, allow fabric to dry completely before packaging.
    h) Handle fabrics as little as possible.

HAIR

1) Investigative considerations
    a) Identify suspect.
    b) Eliminate suspect.
    c) Identify indicators of a struggle (in the fingers of decedent)
    d) Identify activities (e.g., establishing the driver in a questionable traffic accident).
    e) Reconstruct the incident.
    f) An examination of human hair can occasionally reveal the possible race of the individual from whom it came and the part of the body from which it originated.
    g) Human hair can be compared to determine whether or not two samples could have a common origin. The value of laboratory examinations of such specimens will depend on the amount of hair recovered and the characteristics found in the examinations.

2) Collection considerations
    a) Recover all hair present. If possible, use the fingers or tweezers to pick up hair and

place in paper bindles or coin envelopes, which should then be folded and sealed in larger envelopes. Label the outer sealed envelope.

b) If hair is attached, such as in dried blood, or caught in metal or a crack of glass, do not attempt to remove it; rather leave hair intact on the object. If the object is small, mark it, wrap it, and seal it in an envelope. If the object is large, wrap the area containing the hair in paper to prevent loss of hairs during shipment.

c) In rape cases, the victim's pubic region should be combed prior to collecting standards. Obtain known hair samples from the victim, suspect, or any other possible sources for comparison with unknown specimens.

d) The recommended method for collecting head hairs is to have the person from whom they are being collected bend over a large sheet of clean paper and then rub or massage his hands through the hair so that loose hair will fall out on the paper. More should then be gathered by plucking them from representative areas all over the head. A total of 50 to 100 hairs is desired. Do not cut the hair.

e) This same method may be used to collect hairs from other parts of the body. For pubic hair, 30 to 60 hairs are required. When a person is a suspect, collect hair from all parts of the body even though you may be interested only in hair from the head at that particular time.

f) To prevent cross-contamination (or the appearance that cross-contamination may have occurred), never transport the live rape victim and the suspect of the rape in the same police or other official vehicle. Likewise, prevent the possibility of cross-contamination between victim and suspect by considering other common areas (e.g., the interview room) to avoid until such time as the collection of personal evidence has occurred.

g) To prevent cross-contamination, seriously consider denying access at crime scenes to detectives not wearing protective clothing and having those detectives conduct crime-scene canvassing and entering other people's homes.

FINGERNAIL SCRAPINGS

1) Investigative considerations
    a) Maybe indicating evidence of a struggle
    b) Maybe validating testimony
    c) Maybe identifying a possible suspect
    d) Maybe facilitating serology/DNA processing

2) Collection consideration
    a) Place in a paper envelope.

BONES

1) Investigative considerations
    a) Distinguising between human and animal
    b) Maybe assisting in identification of individual
    c) Maybe assisting in identification of weapon (e.g., tool marks, impressions, caliber dimensions)
    d) Maybe assisting in determining origin of bones (e.g., war trophies)
    e) Maybe helping to establish time frame since death.

2) Collection consideration
    a) Place bones in a cardboard box.

CIGARETTE BUTTS

1)   Investigative considerations
          a) Serology/DNA testing for identification of smoker
          b) Manufacturer of cigarette

2)   Collection consideration
          a) Place in paper envelope.

CONDOM EVIDENCE

1)   Investigative considerations
          a) Manufacturers produce condoms using a variety of materials. In addition, such
             substances as particulants added to the condom to prevent the condom from sticking
             to itself, lubricants, and spermicide used in the manufacturing of condoms may be able
             to link to a particular brand with a suspect.
                i) For example, a condom wrapper found at the scene may contain the suspect's
                   print. The composition of this particular brand of condom may have been
                   recovered on the victim. In addition, condom trace evidence may also provide
                   the following:
                      (1) Evidence of penetration
                      (2) Links to acts of serial sexual predators

2)   Collection considerations
          a) Anyone responsible for the collection of rape evidence—from the crime-scene
             technician to the forensic pathologist collecting the rape kit material—must use
             powderless gloves.
                i) The same particulants used to keep the condom material from sticking to itself
                   may be used for the same purpose with examination gloves.
                ii) After collecting the evidence, package the gloves used to process the evidence
                   separately and submit them with the other collected evidence.
                      (1) The forensic laboratory will verify that the gloves did not leave behind
                         any particulates.
          b) Make every effort to recover the foil packet previously containing the condom.
                i) Wipe the inside with a clean cotton swab. The traces on this swab will serve as
                   the standard for comparison with traces recovered from the victim and the
                   suspect.
          c) Victim examination
                i) Additional swabs should be taken for the collection of condom trace material.
                ii) Swabbings should occur in the same areas as the rape swabbings. In addition,
                   swab for condom trace material on the external genitalia of the victim.
          d) Suspect examination
                i) If a suspect is identified within a few hours of the incident, identifiable traces
                   from the victim or the condom may be discerned.

3)   Legal considerations
          a) When preparing a warrant to search a suspect's possessions or residence, be sure to
             include condoms.

FIBERS AND THREADS

1)   Investigative considerations

a) Match fracture (torn edge) to suspect fabric.

b) Identifyf manufacturer.

c) Similarities of origin with suspect sample. Fibers and threads can also be compared with suspect's clothing to determine whether or not they could have come from this clothing.

d) Such evidence is often found in fabric abrasions or caught in torn materials or other areas on hit-and-run vehicles. In some burglary cases, it may be found caught in torn screens, broken glass, or other locations.

e) Examination can usually determine the type or color of fiber, as well as sometimes revealing the type of garment or fabric from which they originated.

2) Collection consideration

a) If threads or large fibers are found, they can often be picked up with the fingers and placed in a paper bindle and later in a coin envelope, which can be sealed and marked. Never place loose fibers directly into a mailing envelop, since they can be lost from this type of envelope.

b) If the fibers are short or few in number, and if it is possible to do so, wrap the area or the entire item containing the fibers in paper and send the whole exhibit to the laboratory.

c) Pick up fibers on tape only if the laboratory in your jurisdiction allows it and gives you its requirements. When fibers or threads are recovered, always send all clothing of persons from which they might have originated to the laboratory for comparison purposes.

d) In sex offenses, assaults, and various other cases, it may be possible to indicate or demonstrate contact between two individuals or between one individual and some other object (such as a car seat) by comparing fibers. Such examinations are only of value when it is known no contact occurred between the two individuals or an individual and some other object prior to, or subsequent to, the offense.

   i) Extra care must be taken to keep each article of clothing of each individual or other object separate.

   ii) Each garment should be laid on a clean sheet of paper, marked as an exhilit, and then rolled up separately. If the clothing of one subject touches the clothing of another, or if it is laid down on a table or placed on a car seat that has been contacted by the clothing of the other suspect, the comparisons may be of no value.

CLOTHING

1) Investigative considerations

a) Blood-spatter interpretation

b) Gunpowder residue that may indicate the distance shot was fired from.

c) Traced to a particular individual, thereby identifying that individual

d) Identification of an accelerant

2) Collection consideration

a) In most cases, allow to air-dry and place in paper bag.

b) In suspected arson cases place clothing items in separate metal cans.

c) May wish to consider removal of clothing on deceased individual if bloodstain analysis is a consideration. Transporting and storage of the decedent may adversely affect later interpretation of the clothing spatter due to bleeding and pulling of the blood.

SHOES

1) Investigative considerations
      a) Possible identification of owner
      b) Possible link to scene due to footprints, serology, or trace materials (soil, fiber, etc.)

2) Collection consideration
      a) Place in cardboard box.

FABRIC

1) Investigative considerations:
      a) Fracture match with evidence for victim, scene or involving suspect
      b) Manufacturer
      c) Origin of item
      d) Link to a particular crime scene

2) Collection consideration
      a) In a paper bag or envelope (air-dry)

ROPE

1) Investigative considerations
      a) Fracture match of suspected rope
      b) Identify manufacturer
      c) Adhering fibers a possible source of identification
      d) Type of knot (if present) possibly of a particular work group

2) Collection consideration
      a) Place in a paper bag.

GLASS

1) Investigative considerations
      a) Fracture match
      b) Determination of type of object causing break
      c) Sequence development
      d) Direction of breakage
      e) Windows are frequently broken in burglaries, headlights are broken in hit-and-run cases, and bottles or other objects may break or leave fragments on personal belongings of suspects involved in various types of crimes.

2) Recovery of evidence samples
      a) Shoes and clothing of suspects or other objects contaminated with glass should be wrapped in paper and submitted to the laboratory for examination.
      b) All glass found at hit-and-run scenes should be recovered.
          i) The search should not be limited to the point of impact, because headlight glass
          may be dispersesd for some distance as the car leaves the crime scene.
          ii) Glass from different locations should be kept in different containers.

iii) All glass should be collected because more than one type may be present. In addition, if just a few representative samples are saved, individual pieces that could be physically matched with glass remaining in the headlight shell of the suspected vehicle may be overlooked.

c) Place small glass fragments in paper bindles and later in coin envelopes, pillboxes, or film canisters that can be marked and completely sealed.

d) Place large glass fragments in boxes. Separate individual pieces with cotton or tissue to prevent breakage and damaged edges during shipment. Seal and mark the box containing them.

3) Standards for comparison
    a) Windows
        i) If the broken window is small, send the whole window or all glass remaining to the laboratory.
        ii) If the window is large, recover several samples from different areas of the window.
        iii) If the evidence glass is large enough to physically match the broken edges or compare the fracture lines, hackle marks, surface abrasions, or contamination, the whole broken window is necessary.
    b) Auto glass—auto headlights
        i) All glass remaining in the shell should be recovered.
            (1) If it is suspected that new glass has been installed, this should be removed and a careful examination made for small chips remaining in the shell from the previous lens that is broken. In such cases, also submit the new lens to the laboratory.
    c) Other glass
        i) When bottles or other glass objects are broken, recover all remaining glass.
    d) Headlights and taillights of motor vehicles
        i) As part of the investigation of vehicle accidents, it may be important to determine whether a headlight or taillight was illuminated at the time the light was broken.
        ii) Recovery of the filaments is of primary importance. These are quite small, so their location may require a careful search.
            (1) If recovered, the filaments should be placed in a paper bindle or a small pillbox sealed with tape.
            (2) Whether or not the large filaments are located, all remaining parts of the lamp socket, glass envelope, or sealed-beam headlight unit should be wrapped in paper and saved for laboratory study.

PAINT

1) Investigative considerations
    a) Paint evidence is frequently encountered in hit-and-run cases, on tools used by burglars, and occasionally in other types of cases.
    b) This may assist in identifying the particular vehicle involved in incident.
    c) This may be used for a fracture match for identification purposes.
    d) This may identify an object.
    e) This may identify a manufacturer.

2) Collection considerations

a) Hit-and-run cases

  i) Paint may be transferred to clothing of pedestrian victims. Examine all areas, with particular attention being paid to areas showing pressure glaze, tears, or other contact.

  ii) If found, do not remove the paint, but mark the garment, carefully wrap it by rolling it in paper, and send it to the laboratory.

  iii) Such paint will at least show the color of part of the responsible car.

    (1) It must be remembered, however, that many modern cars have more than one color and the paint transferred represents only the color of the particular area on the car that made contact with the victim.

  iv) Rarely will an examination of paint transfer on clothing indicate the make and model of the vehicle involved, since only portions of the top oxidized layer on the cars are usually transferred. In addition, many vehicles are repainted using colors and types of paint that may be different from those specified by the automobile manufacturer.

    (1) The color and type of paint selected by the car owner for repainting his vehicle may also be the same as that used by a different automobile manufacturer, which could cause confusion in the search for the responsible car.

  v) Sometimes whole chips of paint will be transferred to the clothing. If these flakes contain several layers, and in particular if they come from a repainted car, such evidence may have great value when the responsible vehicle is located.

    (1) Chips of paint may also be found on the ground near the point of impact in some cases.

  vi) Obtain samples for comparison from all areas showing fresh damage on suspected vehicles.

    (1) This is very important, since the paint may be different in type or composition in different areas, even if the color is the same.

    (2) If the paint can be flaked off by bending the metal slightly, remove it in this manner. If not, scrape or chip the paint off, using a clean knife blade. Carefully wipe the blade before collecting each sample.

    (3) Collect all layers down to the metal.

    (4) Place each sample in a separate container.

  vii) Cross transfers of paint commonly occur in hit and-run cases of two or more vehicles.

    (1) If loose paint chips are found, attempt to remove and place them in a paper bindle. If, however, the transfers are smeared on the surfaces, flake off chips or scrape paint from the vehicle, including the transferred paint, as well as the top layer of paint originally on the car.

    (2) Keep all transfers recovered from different areas in separate containers.

    (3) Do NOT place samples directly into envelopes — place into paper bindles first.

  viii) When cross-transfers occur, always collect contaminated samples from each vehicle from areas immediately adjacent to each transfer collected. This is very important because such specimens permit the laboratory to distinguish between the transferred paint and the paint originally present on the vehicle.

b) Burglary-related homicide cases

  i) Tools used to gain entry into building, safes, or other places often contain traces of paint, as well as other substances, such as plastic, safe insulation, etc. Care must be taken that such traces are not lost.

(1) If such transfers may be present, wrap the end of the tool containing the material in clean paper and seal with tape to prevent loss.

(2) In no case should attempts be made to set the tool into marks or impressions found. If this is done, transfers of paint or material can occur, and any traces found later will have no significance as evidence.

ii) Collect specimens of paint from all areas that the tools may have contacted at the crime scene.

(1) These samples should include all layers present.

(2) Do not destroy the tool mark in collecting the paint. If possible, cut out around the mark and send it to the laboratory.

iii) The tool itself may contain paint or other coatings, tracings of which may be left at the crime scene. A careful search should be made for such matters, particularly in each tool mark.

3)   Collection and preservation of paint specimens

a) Keep all samples collected in separate containers.

b) Small paper bindles can be used to collect and hold many paint samples.

i) One satisfactory method is to tape one side of the bindle to the side of the vehicle, building, or safe just under the area where the sample is to be collected.

ii) By holding the bindle open with one hand and using a clean knife blade, you can scrape paint loose and into the bindle.

iii) Remove the bindle from the collection source. Fold the paper bindle to retain the specimen. Scotch tape is only used to keep bindle secure in collecting the specimen.

iv) Place the specimen in a coin or mailing envelope, which can be marked and sealed.

v) Scotch tape can be used to seal the bindle, but such containers should never be stapled.

c) Glass vials or other suitable containers are used only as a last resort.

d) Never place paint directly into envelopes unless large pieces are enclosed.

i) Most envelopes have unsealed cracks in the corners, which can result in loss or contamination.

FLAMMABLE FLUIDS/ARSON MATERIAL

1)   Investigative considerations

a) Accelerants contained within may indicate that arson has occurred, not an accidental fire.

b) The search for flammable fluids in arson cases should include a thorough examination of the entire fire scene.

i) This should extend to areas where no burning occurs, since flammable fluids may have been placed in other locations where ignition failed.

c) To help in the effort to identify the perpetrator of the arson:

i) Fingerprints may be developed on accelerant materials and points of entrances and exits at the fire with a suspect.

ii) A suspect may be linked to the scene through an accelerant found on the suspect's clothing or fingerprints found on the discarded flammable material container.

iii) A suspect may be identified through witnesses who saw him buying the flammable material shortly before the fire.

d) Reconstruction of what occurred can be developed through cause and origin experts.

e) Testimony concerning witnesses may be refuted or validated based on arson evidence processing.

f) It is possible, in many cases, to isolate flammable fluids from various, partly burned articles through gas chromatographic analysis and other studies to determine the type of flammable fluid present.

    i) Normally, however, the manufacturer or brand name of the material cannot be determined.

g) The type of accelerant used can be determined.

    i) It is possible, in many cases, to isolate flammable fluids from various, partly burned articles through gas chromatographic analysis and other studies to determine the type of flammable fluid present.

    ii) Normally, however, the manufacturer or brand name of the material cannot be determined.

h) Traces of flammable fluid may be found in cans at the fire scene in arson cases.

    i) Mattresses, rugs, upholstery, wallboard, and other objects at the scene may also contain fluids, which can be separated and identified in the laboratory, even though these objects are partly burned.

    ii) Wood upon which such fluids have been poured and ignited may still contain detectable traces of the liquid if the wood has not been completely charred by the fire.

        (1) Even where a large, hot fire has occurred, traces of such liquid are sometimes found where they have seeped into the ground through cracks in the floor or flowed under baseboards and sills.

2) Collection considerations

a) Small samples of soil, wood, cloth, paper, etc., should be placed in small, clean metal cans and sealed immediately to prevent loss of additional volatile components by evaporation.

b) Large pieces of wood, upholstery, wallboard, and similar exhibits that will not fit in cans should be placed in heat-sealed KAPAK plastic.

c) If volatile liquids are found in open containers, pour a small amount of the material into a clean glass vial with an airtight seal so no loss will occur. Do not use any rubber-lined lids or plastic containers.

d) When the exhibits themselves can be marked, this should be done. In all cases the package or container should be marked.

e) Samples of flammable fluids normally present at fire scenes should also be submitted for comparison with any material recovered from partly burned substances.

f) Samples of flammable fluids in the possession of any suspects should be submitted for comparison purposes.

    i) This includes any clothing, rags, or other materials that have suspicious stains or odors.

    ii) These should be packaged in the same manner as materials recovered at the fire scene.

FIREARMS EVIDENCE

1) Investigative considerations

a) Identification of suspect weapon

b) Elimination as potential weapon

c) Type of weapon involved

d) Range determination

e) Reconstruction of incident

2)   Collection consideration

        a) Never submit a loaded gun to the lab unless it is delivered in person. Unfired cartridges may be left in the magazine of a weapon, provided the magazine is removed from the gun. A firearm with the cartridge in the chamber should never be shipped by any method, even if the weapon is not cocked or on safety.

        b) Never clean the bore, chamber, or cylinder before submitting a firearm, and never attempt to fire the gun before it is examined in the laboratory.

        c) Never pick up a weapon by placing a pencil or other object in the end of the barrel.

        d) Record serial number, make, model, and caliber of the weapon, and mark the weapon in some inconspicuous manner that does not detract from its value before sending it to the lab. Marking firearms is important, since duplicate serial numbers are sometimes found on different guns of the same make and general type. Do not confuse model numbers or patent numbers with serial numbers.

        e) Place weapons in strong cardboard or wooden boxes, pack them well to prevent shifting of guns in transit.

        f) Rifles or shotguns should not be taken apart.

        g) If blood or any other material that may pertain to an investigation is present on the gun, place a clean paper around the gun and seal it with tape to prevent movement of the gun and loss of the sample during shipment.

        h) If the gun is to be examined for latent fingerprints, use procedures outlined later in this manual.

BULLETS

1)   Investigative considerations

        a) Type of weapon (revolver, semiautomatic, rifle, etc.)

        b) Was it used in the crime?

        c) Possible link to a particular weapon

2)   Collection considerations

        a) Never mark bullets.

        b) Wrap recovered bullets in paper and seal in separate labeled pillboxes or envelopes.

        c) Submit all evidence bullets recovered to the lab. A conclusive identification may be possible on only one of several bullets recovered even if they all appear to be in good condition.

        d) Do not attempt to clean recovered bullets before sending them to the lab.

            i) Bullets recovered from a body should be air-dried and wrapped in paper.

            ii) Washing may destroy trace evidence.

CARTRIDGE CASES

1)   Investigative considerations

        a) Type of weapon used

        b) Marks from firing pin, ejectors, or chamber may be matched to a particular weapon (IBIS, DrugFire).

2)   Collection considerations

a) Wrap recovered cartridge cases in and seal in separate labeled pillboxes or envelopes.

b) Fired shotgun shells may be marked either on the inside or outside of the paper or plastic portion of the shell.

c) If an examination is required to determine whether a shot shell or cartridge case was fired by a specific weapon, submit the weapon and all recovered unfired ammunition.

d) Submit all evidence cartridge cases or shotgun shells recovered to the lab.
   Some cases contain more identifying details than others.

e) Wrap each cartridge in paper to prevent damaging the breechblock, firing pin, or other markings by contact with other cartridge cases.

   i) Place wrapped cartridge cases in envelopes or pillboxes.

   ii) Label and seal container.

AMMUNITION

1) Collection considerations:

   a) Always attempt to recover unused ammunition for comparison purposes when firearms are obtained as evidence.

   i) If it is not in the weapon itself, subjects often have additional ammunition in their cars, clothing, houses, or other locations.

   ii) It may be important for test purposes to duplicate exactly the make, type, and age of the ammunition used in the crime. Other ammunition in the suspect's possession may be identical to that fired during the crime.

   b) Unfired ammunition should not be marked. The box with the ammunition may be marked without marking every round in the box.

BUCKSHOT OR PELLETS

1) Investigative consideration

   a) Is it consistent with other ammo found in suspect's possession?

2) Collection consideration

   a) Put it in cardboard box.

SHOTGUN SHELL

1) Investigative consideration

   a) Identification of the gauge

   b) Marks from the firing pin or ejector maybe matched to a particular weapon

2) Collection consideration

   a) Put it in a paper bag.

WADDING

1) Investigative considerations

   a) Gauge of shotgun

   b) Make of shell

   c) Type of powder

2) Collection consideration

   a) Put it in a paper envelope.

POWDER AND SHOT PATTERN

1)   Investigative considerations
          a) For gunpowder or shot pattern tests to have significance, it is essential to obtain
              ammunition identical in make, type, and age to that used at the crime scene. This
              duplicate ammunition is necessary for firing in the weapon in question to determine
              the distance of the muzzle of the weapon from the victim or other object at the time
              the questioned bullet was fired.

2)   Collection consideration
          a) Submit clothing or other material showing evidence of gunpowder residue or shot
              holes to the lab.
                  i) The clothing should be carefully wrapped in clean paper and folded as little as
                      possible to prevent dislodging powder particles.
                  ii) Photographs of the pattern will not suffice, since in most instances microscopic
                      examination and chemical tests must be conducted on the exhibits themselves.
                  iii) Package each item separately.

GUNSHOT RESIDUE

1)   Investigative considerations
          a) Determine if weapon was fired.
          b) Determine range of fire.
          c) Determine type of ammunition.
          d) Validate witness statements.

2)   Collection considerations
          a) Gunshot residue (GSR) is extremely fragile evidence and should be collected as soon
              as possible (preferably within 3 hours of the discharge of firearm).
          b) Usually GSR kits come prepackaged with directions.
          c) In the case of live subjects, if more than 6 hours have passed or if the subject has
              washed his hands, it is unlikely that meaningful results will be obtained.
          d) If a body is to be sampled, whenever possible, GSR collection should be
              performed prior to moving the body. If this is not possible, protect the hands with
              paper bags.

SERIAL NUMBER RESTORATION

1)   In many cases, obliterated serial numbers can be restored if not too much metal has been
      removed in erasing the number.
2)   If the original number can be restored, a crime lab should restamp the number on the
      involved firearm. If it cannot be restored, a new number is usually assigned to the firearm.

TOOL MARKS

1)   Investigative considerations
          a) A tool mark is any impression, scratch, gouge, cut, or abrasion made when a tool is
              brought into contact with another object.
                  i) Tool marks can take the form of a negative impression (stamping type) or
                      abrasion (friction type) mark. Some marks are combination of both features.

b) Special precautions
    i) Doors, windows, or other openings with hinged or sliding doors should not be opened, closed, or handled in any way that might compromise latent fingerprints (these usually occur near the points of entry or exit).
    ii) Investigators should also take special note of any broken, forced, or cut locks, latches, or bolts in the immediate area.
c) Identification of possible object
    i) Fracture match
    ii) Trace evidence matching on possible suspect object
d) Tool marks are encountered most frequently in burglary cases but may also be found in other types of crimes.
e) The evidence consists of striations or impressions left by tools on objects at the crime scene and various types of tools found in the possession of suspects.
f) In other cases, it is possible by means of physical and other comparisons to prove that parts of tools left at crime scenes were broken from damaged tools found in the possession of suspects.
g) Lab examinations, and comparisons of tools from a suspect with tool marks recovered from a crime scene, can often provide conclusive evidence to link a suspect to a specific crime.
h) In some instances, it is also possible to prove that marks of various types on tools were produced by objects that they contacted at crime scene.

2)   Photography
    a) Two types of photographs are needed for courtroom identification:
        i) An overall photo depicting the entire object bearing the tool mark
        ii) A close-up photo showing the detail of the tool mark that is for identification and orientation only and cannot be used for actual comparisons
    b) Photographs should show the physical location and arrangement of the door, window, or other item bearing the mark. These can reveal the direction of tool use and whether the tool is physically capable of making the mark. A scale or ruler should also be included in these photographs.

3)   Trace evidence
    a) After carefully considering the possibility of latent print recovery, examine tool marks carefully for the potential presence of any trace evidence.
        i) Examine carefully for any loosely adhering particles of evidence.
            (1) If present, trace material may be handled in two ways:
                (a) The trace material can be removed and separately packaged.
                    (i) Trace evidence removed from the object surface.
                        1. On painted surfaces bearing a tool mark, sample scrapings of the paint should also be submitted to the lab. Paint may not be readily seen adhering to the tool; however, microscopic examination of the tool may reveal minute particles having evidentiary value.
                        2. When a tool mark is on a surface that cannot be removed entirely, such as on a large, heavy metal object, samples of the metal should be obtained and submitted as reference standards. Particles of metal may adhere to the tool in

addition to paint, and both may be analyzed and compared.

    (ii) Flakes of adhering paint might be lost from the tool while it is in transit to the lab; therefore, a plastic bag should be taped over the end of an object to prevent loss or contamination of trace evidence.

(b) The trace evidence can be carefully avoided while fingerprint powder is applied.

    (i) Keep in mind that applying and removing powders can destroy trace evidence.

    (ii) Tool mark evidence should be packaged so as not to subject it to damage or loss of trace evidence.

4)   Preservation and packaging of tools

    a) All areas on recovered tools that contain transferred paint, building material, or other contamination should be wrapped in paper and packaged to prevent the prying blades or cutting edges from contacting any other surface or object.

5)   No testing with tools

    a) Attempts should never be made to fit tools into questioned marks or to make test marks prior to lab examination.

      i) If done, the questioned mark or tool may be altered, and this may make any lab examination worthless.

      ii) In addition, traces of transferred paint or other stains on the tool may be lost or additional material may be transferred to the tool.

6)   Preservation of tool marks

    a) Whenever possible, submit the whole object containing tool marks to the lab instead of just removing the area containing the mark.

      i) If this is not possible, carefully photograph and sketch the area containing the mark. Although this photograph won't allow the lab to perform a tool mark comparison with the tool, it will assist the lab in determining how the mark was made so that test marks can be more easily made.

    b) Any items removed as evidence should be clearly marked with case number, initials, and date of removal. The evidence should also be marked to show the inside or outside; top, or bottom; and the surface area bearing the tool mark.

      i) Use a felt-tip pen or include a separate drawing with the submitted evidence.

      ii) Many objects bearing tool marks that are detached on forced entry can be submitted directly. This includes the following:

        (1) Segments of window or door molding

        (2) Window or door sill, latches, bolts, locks or doorknobs

          (a) Where doorknobs are twisted, note whether anything obstructs access to the knob from either side (e.g., posts, door set-back).

          (b) Any small removable item (such as a doorknob, latch plate, or lock) should be marked by the investigator showing the top and front of the item as it was positioned before removal.

    c) A person who has had considerable experience in this work can make casts of tool marks. Poor casts are useless for comparison purposes and some marks will be damaged if improper methods are used.

      i) If an actual item cannot be submitted for tool mark examination a cast can be made.

          (1) A suitable casting material is Mikrosil. Two speeds of hardener are supplied in the casting kit. The *slow* hardener is suitable for normal casting. The *fast* hardener is used for casting in very cold climates. Complete mixing of the casting material and hardener is essential.

              (a) A properly mixed portion will be workable for about 1 to 2 minutes, and the cast can be removed in about 10 minutes.

              (b) A hardened Mikrosil cast cannot be permanently marked with a pen; therefore, the cast must be placed in a suitable container that can be appropriately marked with item number, location, date and name of person making the cast.

d) Pack the object containing tool marks so that no alteration or damage will occur during shipment.

      i) Small objects should be wrapped with clean paper and placed in envelopes or boxes, while important areas on larger objects can be protected with paper.

      ii) Whole large objects can be packed in cartons or crates if they are not delivered in person.

TIRE TREADS

1) Investigative considerations

    a) Identification of suspect vehicle

    b) Reconstruction of events, including speed involved

2) Collection consideration

    a) Photographs, measurements, and casting

CONTROLLED SUBSTANCES AND MEDICAL PREPARATIONS

1) Investigative considerations

    a) Determine the type of drug that may be involved.

    b) Determine the effect the drug has with regard to the circumstances surrounding the death.

    c) Is the drug responsible for causing the subject's death?

2) Collection considerations

    a) Each sample of material recovered should be placed in a paper container, which can be sealed and marked. Be sure to properly seal it; loose material, particularly in the case of marijuana, can leak and spill. Some drugs, such as PCP, should be packaged in heat-sealed KAPAK bags.

    b) Medicinal preparations found in prescription boxes or bottles should be left in the containers, which can be sealed and marked. Place in plastic see-through bags, if possible.

    c) Most controlled substances and common drugs can be identified through chemical tests.

    d) Many pills, tablets, and other medical preparations are very difficult to analyze and identify unless either large quantities are available for testing or some clues are present about the general type of material they contain.

    e) In all cases where prescriptions are involved and the drugstore and prescription numbers are known, a check of possible container content should be made at the drug store named on the label.

       i) Determine if there are any other prescription issued by this pharmacy.

    f) All evidence of this nature should be brought to the lab in a sealed package.

QUESTIONED DOCUMENTS

1)   Questioned material to be submitted

        a) All questioned documents involved in a particular investigation should be submitted to the lab for examination. This is important because questioned documents are identified by a comparison of similarities, plus an absence of divergences or dissimilarities. To make an identification, sufficient handwriting, typewriting, or other evidence must be available on which to base an opinion. This means that all questioned material is needed, as well as sufficient exemplars or known specimens.

           i) Exemplars

              (1) It is very important to have sufficient handwriting samples for comparison with the questioned document. One or two signatures on a suspect's driver's license or a draft card, in many cases, do not contain enough individual characteristics on which to base a conclusion. In some instances, such an examination may substantiate a suspicion, and this should be considered as an investigation lead. To support this, it is necessary to obtain and examine additional standards.

              (2) Collected specimens that were made in business transactions (such as receipts, promissory notes, credit and employment applications, letters, booking card, and fingerprint card signatures) are writings that, in most cases, represent the individual's most normal writing.

                  (a) It is significant in many cases that these writings be of the same date as the questioned document.

                  (b) It is important to obtain request specimens from a suspect at the first interview; the suspect may be uncooperative at a later date.

              (3) The conditions surrounding the preparation of the questioned document should be duplicated as nearly as possible when the request exemplars are obtained. If yellow-lined paper and blue ink were used to produce the questioned document, the same or similar color and type of paper and instrument should be used.

                  (a) If the suspect document is a threatening letter and the note is either handwritten or block-lettered, the same style should be requested from the writer.

                  (b) Have the subject write his name and addresses several times and a brief personal history. This should be removed and another heet of paper furnished.

                  (c) Dictate the exact words and numbers that appear on the questioned document. This should be done at least 12 times, removing the specimens from the writer's view as they are produced.

                  (d) If it is a check case, the specimens should be taken on blank checks or slips of paper of the same or appropriate size.

              (4) The number of specimens necessary for an identification in any

specific case cannot be determined; therefore, at least 12 specimens should be obtained for each questioned document.

(5) When securing typewritten exemplars, several copies of the questioned documents should be made on the suspected machine using light, medium, and heavy touches.

    (a) At least one copy should be made with the ribbon removed from the machine or set on stencil, and the keys allowed to strike directly on a sheet of new carbon paper, which should be inserted on top of the paper used for the specimen.

    (b) This provides clear-cut exemplars of any machine's type face, showing disfigurations in type characters. Always type the exemplars on the same type and color of paper as that used on the questioned document.

2)   Preservation of questioned documents

    a) Under no circumstances should either the questioned document or the exemplars be marked, defaced, or altered.

        i) New folds should not be made, nor should marks or notes be placed on such material.

        ii) Personal marks for identification purposes should be made as small as possible on the back or other area of the document where no handwriting or typewriting is present.

    b) Whenever possible, all documents should be protected by placing them in cellophane or plastic envelopes.

3)   Shipment of evidence

    a) Evidence sent to the lab by mail must be sent by certified or registered mail. If there is a massive amount of material, it may be sent some other way, but the package must always be sealed.

CHARRED DOCUMENTS

1)   Where examination and decipherment of charred paper are involved, great care must be taken to prevent any additional crumbling or breaking apart of the burned material.

2)   Normally the material should be placed on top of loose cotton in a box and delivered in person to the lab.

    a) No matter how it is packaged, such material will be damaged if attempts are made to ship it by mail.

OTHER QUESTIONED DOCUMENT EVIDENCE

1)   In addition to handwriting and typewriting comparisons and the decipherment of charred documents, the lab can conduct many other related examinations. These include but are not limited to the following:

    a) Restoration or decipherment of altered, obliterated, or erased writing

    b) Comparison of check protectors and rubber stamps with questioned printing

    c) Identification of embossed or indented writing or typing

    d) Comparison of paper and such commercially printed material as checks, coupons, and receipts

e) Physical matching of cut or torn paper of various types

f) Problems relating to and identification of inks

LATENT FINGERPRINTS

1) Marking of latent fingerprint evidence
   a) All such evidence should be marked in some distinctive manner, as is the case with any other type of physical evidence. Take precautions when marking evidence not to damage or destroy potential latent fingerprints.
   b) Lifted, developed latents should also be marked or sealed in marked envelopes.
   c) Photograph developed latents with and without identifying markings and scale.

2) Preservation of fingerprint evidence
   a) The primary precaution in all cases is not to add fingerprints to evidence or destroy those already present.
   b) Most fingerprints submitted are on paper, glass, metal, or other smooth-surfaced objects. When articles containing latents must be picked up, touch as little as possible, and then only in areas least likely to contain identifiable latents, such as rough surfaces.
   c) Gloves or handkerchiefs can be used to pick up such exhibits, but avoid any unnecessary contact.
      i) Although using a cloth to pick up exhibits prevents leaving additional prints on the articles, the cloth will frequently wipe off or smear any prints present, unless great care is taken.
   d) Large articles containing latents (e.g., glass, metal articles, firearms) should be placed on wood or heavy cardboard and fastened down with string to prevent shifting and contact with other objects in transit.
      i) Where such evidence is to be examined frequently, use a pegboard on which wooden pegs can be moved as desired to support exhibits and keep them from moving.
      ii) Bottles and glasses may be placed vertically on a board and placed in the bottom of a box. The base of the bottle or glass can be surrounded with nails to hold it in place, and the top can be either inserted through a hole in a piece of cardboard or held in position with a wooden board nailed to the container's lid.
   e) Papers and documents containing latent prints should be placed individually in a cellophane or manila envelope.
      i) Such a container can be sandwiched between two sheets of stiff cardboard, wrapped, and placed in a box for mailing.

SHOEPRINT AND TIRE TREAD EXAMINATIONS

1) Examination consideration
   a) Shoeprint or tire tread impressions are routinely left at crime scenes.
   b) These impressions are retained on surfaces in two-dimensional and three-dimensional forms.
   c) Almost all impressions, including partial impressions, have value for forensic comparisons.
   d) The examination of detailed shoeprint and tire tread impressions often results in the positive identification of the suspect(s)' shoe(s) or tire(s) from the suspect(s)' vehicle(s).

2)   A complete examination consists of two main functions:
           a) The recovery process
                   i) Including the discovery and preservation of the prints
           b) The identification process
                   i) Involving evaluations, comparisons, and findings related to the recovered
                      impression.

3)   To avoid leaving fingerprints at scenes, criminals have learned to wear gloves or wipe down areas
       they may have touched. But almost all criminals will also come into some contact with a scene
       because they must come into contact with the floor with their feet. What they leave behind is
       footwear impressions.
           a) When a crime scene is not properly processed, this type of impression evidence is often
              overlooked or destroyed.
           b) Proper processing of a scene may provide evidence proving that a suspect was at the
              crime scene.

4)   Why are footwear impressions overlooked?
           a) Not believing that the impressions can be found at the scene after people have walked
              over the scene
           b) Incomplete searches of the crime scene
           c) Weather conditions
                   i) In some cases where weather could adversely affect footwear evidence, the first
                      officer on the scene may place boxes, cones, etc., over the impressions until the
                      crime-scene investigator arrives.
           d) The impression being intentionally destroyed

5)   Crime-scene footwear and tire tread evidence
           a) There are two forms of footwear evidence:
                   i) Impressions
                       (1) An impression is a three-dimensional item found in a soft material
                           such as mud, snow, sand, etc.
                   ii) Prints
                       (1) A print is a transferred image made on a solid surface. The print
                           deposit may be established if the solid surface contains dust, powder,
                           or another type of medium.

6)   Like latent fingerprints, footwear evidence is classified into three categories:
           a) Visible prints
                   i) When someone steps onto a surface that is covered by some material, the
                      footwear or foot may become contaminated. When that contaminated foot
                      or footwear object steps onto a clean surface, it may leave behind a visible
                      print. This print is visible with the unaided eye.
                       (1) Contaminated substances can include blood, grease, oil, or water.
                   ii) You should attempt to photograph this visible print before trying any lifting
                      method. If the footwear evidence is composed of dust, a dust electrostatic lifter
                      (DELK) can also be used.
           b) Plastic prints
                   i) When a person wearing footwear steps onto a soft surface, he may leave behind
                      a three-dimensional plastic print. The soft surface may be mud, snow, wet
                      sand, or dirt.

                  (1) Processing involves photographing and casting.

        c) Latent prints

            i) When the foot or footwear object comes into contact with a smooth surface, it may leave behind a footprint similar to a latent fingerprint. This print can be processed in the same way as a latent fingerprint.

            ii) As when processing a latent fingerprint, various development chemicals and powders used in conjunction with a forensic light source maximize the development of the latent footwear print.

7)   There are four basic methods of recording footwear impressions at the crime scene:

        a) Photography

        b) Documentation/sketching

        c) Casting

        d) Lifting

8)   Searching the crime scene

        a) To process a death scene competently and successfully, identifying footwear evidence has to be one of the your first considerations upon arrival at the scene.

9)   Recovering the original evidence

        a) Submit the evidence bearing the original impression to the lab whenever possible.

        b) If the evidence cannot be submitted to the lab, use the following techniques to recover the evidence.

            i) Outdoor footwear evidence

                (1) Photograph

                (2) Cast of the foot impression if it is three-dimensional

                    (a) First consideration should be given to evidence that may become obliterated without quick attention.

            ii) Indoor footwear evidence

                (1) Darken the search area as much as possible.

                (2) Identify footwear patterns by using a strong white light with a directional beam. This beam should be directed over the scene's surface at an oblique angle.

        c) All identified impressions should be photographed, documented, lifted, or cast.

            i) A photograph or lift is two-dimensional. It differs from a cast in that the latter is a three-dimensional structure that can provide a positive reproduction of the footwear.

        d) If an item contains a footwear impression or print, it is better to collect the item from the scene and send it to the lab for processing. It is much easier to work on the evidence under controlled conditions provided by a lab than it is to try to recover a footwear impression at a scene.

        e) Many latent footwear impressions can be located by using a light source at an oblique angle.

            i) Latent fingerprint powders can be used to build contrast for photographing the print. Do this procedure just as you would process a latent print. After developing and photographing the print, use fingerprint-lifting tape and place the print on a contrasting lift card.

10)   Lifting two-dimensional impressions

a) DELK
    i) Since 1981, DELK has been an excellent tool for the recovery of visible and invisible footwear evidence in dust.
        (1) A typical case may involve a suspect coming into a residence through the roof and stepping onto a table before stepping down to the floor. A DELK applied to the surface of the table should do an excellent job of developing the suspect's shoe print.
    ii) DELK lifts footwear impressions from porous and nonporous surfaces without damaging the impressions. This device works on dry dust or residue impressions on clean surfaces but will not work if the impressions were wet or become wet.
    iii) Lifting an impression allows for the transfer of a two-dimensional residue or dust impression to a lifting film.
    iv) It also allows the impression to be transported to the lab for photography and examination.
    v) Store the electrostatic lifting film.
        (1) Lifted impressions are easily damaged if the film is not properly stored.
        (2) The film has a residual charge that attracts dust and debris and causes the film to cling to another surface.
        (3) To preserve and store the lifting film containing an impression, tape one edge of the film securely in a clean, smooth, quality paper folder, or tape the edges securely in a shallow, photographic paper box.
            (a) Low-grade cardboard boxes (e.g., pizza boxes) should not be used because the residual charge on the film will pull dust from the boxes and contaminate the impression.
            (b) Items that contain a dry-residue footwear impression should not be wrapped or stored in plastic because a partial transfer of the impression to the plastic will occur.
    vi) This method of lifting can be used on a variety of surfaces, including floors, doors, countertops, chairs, fabric, metal, carpet, tile, newspapers, bodies, and tar.
b) Adhesive paper or contact paper lifts
    i) Adhesive or contact paper can be used to transfer a footwear impression from a surface covered by dust or very fine dirt.
    ii) The sticky side of the paper's surface is placed on the impression. This should cause the dust impression to be transferred to the adhesive side of the paper. The paper is then peeled off the surface and photographed.
    iii) To increase contrast, the adhesive or contact paper can be stained with a mixture of 0.05 grams of crystal violet to 500 milliliters of distilled water.
    iv) Placing another clear acetate sheet over the lifted sheet for preservation purposes completes the process.
c) Gelatin and adhesive lifts
    i) Gelatin lifters can be used to lift impressions from porous and nonporous surfaces.
    ii) Black gelatin lifters work well for lifting light-colored dry or wet impressions.
    iii) White gelatin lifters can be used to lift impressions developed with fingerprint powders or impressions dark enough to contrast with a white background.
    iv) Adhesive lifters can only be used to lift impressions from smooth porous and nonporous surfaces.

(1) White adhesive lifters can be used to lift impressions developed with fingerprint powders.

(2) Transparent adhesive lifters can be used to lift impressions developed with fluorescent powders.

(3) Transparent tapes (e.g., 2-inch fingerprint-lifting tape) can also be used to lift powdered impressions if they are transferred to a white card.

TABLE 1: LIFTING MATERIALS (Wade, 1999)

Lift or Technique	Nonporous Dry	Nonporous Wet	Porous Dry	Porous Wet	Comments
Electrostatic	Yes	No	Yes	No	Nondestructive; Useful for searching for latent impressions
White adhesive	Yes	Yes	No	No	Also used with chemical enhancement methods and dark fingerprint powder
Transparent adhesive	Only with fluorescent powder	Only with fluorescent powder	No	No	Do not use on an original impression
White gelatin	Yes, if it contrasts with an impression	Yes, if it contrasts with an impression	Yes, if it contrasts with an impression	Yes, if it contrasts with an impression	Also used with some chemical methods and with fluorescent powder
Black gelatin	Yes	Yes	Yes	Yes	Offers good contrast with most residue

11) Photographing shoeprint and tire tread impressions
   a) Crime-scene rules apply to tthe photographing of footwear patterns. That is, always shoot overall, medium, and close-up shots.
   b) Overall and medium photographs
      i) Demonstrate the location of the footwear evidence in the overall scene. Numbered markers may be used to demonstrate this effect.
         (1) Make sure you use the same number for all your photograph sequences.
         (2) Use ISO 400 color film.
   c) Examination-quality photographs should then be taken to obtain maximum detail for forensic examination.
      i) Examination-quality photographs should be taken directly over the impressions using a tripod and lighting. The FBI Laboratory recommends the following procedure:

(1) A scale should be in every photograph. The purpose of these photographs is to produce a detailed negative that can be enlarged to natural size. These photographs should be taken as follows:

   (a) Place a linear scale (e.g., a ruler) next to and on the same plane as the impression. The scale should always be placed parallel to the side of the shoe, never in the print itself.

   (b) Place a label in the picture to correlate the impression with crime-scene notes and general photographs.

(2) Images should be taken with a 35mm or medium-format film camera.

   (a) Low-cost digital cameras do not provide sufficient image detail for examination-quality photographs.

   (b) Use a manual-focus camera and black-and-white film with an ISO of 400 or less.

(3) Place the camera on a tripod and position it directly over the impression.

   (a) Adjust the height of the camera or adjust the zoom lens so the frame is filled with the impression and scale.

   (b) Position the camera so the film plane is parallel to the impression.

(4) Set the f-stop on f/16 or f/22 for a greater depth of field.

(5) Attach an electronic flash with a long extension cord to the camera.

(6) Block out bright ambient light with a sunscreen to maximize the light from the flash.

(7) Focus on the bottom of the impression, not on the scale. Take an existing- or reflected-light photograph.

(8) Position the flash at a very low angle (10 to 15 degrees) to the impression.

   (a) This will enhance the detail of the impression.

   (b) For consistent exposure, hold the flash at least 5 to 7 feet from the impression. Shoot several exposures, bracketing toward overexposure to obtain maximum image detail.

(9) Take the exposures, move the light to another position, adjust the sun screen, and repeat steps 7 and 8.

12) Photographing impressions in snow

   a) Impressions in snow are difficult to photograph because of lack of contrast.

   b) To increase the contrast, snow impressions can be lightly sprayed with Snow Print Wax, a material used for casting snow impressions, or with other colored spray paint.

      i) The spray can should be held at least 2 to 3 feet from the impression so that the force of the aerosol does not damage the impression.

      ii) A light application of spray should be directed at an angle of about 30 to 45 degrees so that the colored paint only strikes the high points of the impression.

      iii) Highlighted impressions will absorb heat from the sun and should be shielded until photographed and cast to prevent melting.

13) Casting an impression

   a) Three-dimensional impressions should be cast if the print and surface condition are suitable.

   b) Why cast?

      i) The cast provides an actual-sized molding of the subject matter.

ii) The cast gives reproduction of microscopic characteristics.

iii) In deep impressions, the cast gives reproduction of characteristics of the side of outsoles and midsoles of the shoe, which usually are not reproduced in photographs.

iv) Focus or scale problems are eliminated.

v) Provides tangible three-dimensional evidence

vi) Backs up the photographs

c) Casting three-dimensional impressions

i) Casting a three-dimensional impression in soil, sand, or snow is necessary to capture detail for examination.

(1) Dental stone, with a compressive strength of 8,000 psi or greater, should be used for casting all impressions. The compressive strength is listed on the container, along with the proper ratio of powder to water used for mixing.

(2) Dental stone is available through local dental supply houses. Colored dental stone is preferred.

(3) Plaster of paris, modeling plasters, and dental plasters are not hard enough, do not resist abrasion when cleaned, and should not be used.

Mixing Dental Stone in a Bag

- Store dental stone in resoluble plastic bags. An 8 x 12-inch resoluble plastic bag can store 2 pounds of dental-stone powder. With premeasured bags, casting impressions at the crime scene involves only adding water.
- The bag containing the dental-stone powder can be used to mix and pour the dental stone.
- To make a cast, add the appropriate amount of water to the bag and close the top.
- Mix the casting material by vigorously massaging it for 3 to 5 minutes through the bag. Ensure that the material in the corners of the bag is also mixed.
- After mixing, the material should have the consistency of pancake batter.

Mixing Dental Stone in a Bucket or Bowl

- If the impressions are numerous or large, it may be necessary to mix larger quantities of dental stone in a bucket or bowl.
- The dental stone should be slowly added to the water and continuously stirred for 3 to 5 minutes.
- After mixing, the material should have the consistency of pancake batter.

Pouring Dental Stone

- Casting material has sufficient weight and volume to erode and destroy detail if it is poured directly on top of the impression.
- The casting material should be poured on the ground next to the impression, allowing it to flow into the impression.
- The impression should be filled with casting material until it has overflowed.
- If the mixture is too viscous to flow into the impression, vibrate a finger or a small stick on the surface to cause it to flow into the impression.
- Do not put the stick or finger more than 1/4 inch below the surface of the casting material because it can damage the impression.
- Before the cast completely hardens, write the date, the collector's initials, and other identifying information on it.
- The cast should be left undisturbed for at least 20 to 30 minutes in warm weather. In cold weather, the cast should be left undisturbed longer.
- Casts have been destroyed or damaged when lifted too soon.
- If the cast is in sand or loose soil, it should lift easily. Casts in mud or clay may require careful treatment and excavation when being removed.

- Allow the cast to air-dry for at least 48 hours. Package the cast in paper, not in plastic. An examiner should clean the cast.

    D) Casting in water
        i) Place a form around the impression, making sure the frame is large enough to come above the waterline.
            (1) Be careful not to place the form so close to the impression that it risks distorting it.
        ii) Remove any debris from the surface of the water.
        iii) Lightly sprinkle the dental-stone material over the area of the impression, about 1 inch, allowing it to settle.
        iv) Prepare a mixture of dental stone that is slightly thicker.
        v) Place the mixture into the frame by scooping.
        vi) Allow 60 minutes for drying.
        vii) Remove and air-dry 48 hours.
   c) Casting in snow
        i) Place a form around the impression.
        ii) Spray Snow Print Wax over the impression and allow it to set up for about 10 minutes.
            (1) If Snow Print Wax is not available, talcum powder or gray primer spray can be used, but the pouring must be done very carefully.
        iii) Prepare a mixture of dental stone using very cold water.
        iv) Pour the dental stone onto the impression very carefully.
        v) Cover the impression with a box and allow the cast to dry for about 60 minutes.
        vi) Remove and air-dry for 48 hours.

PLANTS

1)   Investigative consideration
        a) Establish time frame involving dumped or buried bodies.

2)   Collection consideration
        a) Keep moist. Package in a plastic bag.
        b) Quickly transfer to a forensic botanist.

At a skeleton recovery scene, an athletic shoe still containing a sock with foot bones was found. The shoe had a small tree growing through it. A forensic botanist was able to give some insight about time frame involved for this particular vegetation to have evolved. This information allowed the death investigator to start a search for any person who had been missing at least since the time the tree began growing through the shoe.

EVIDENCE COLLECTION EQUIPMENT

The following contains a list of evidence-collection supplies recommended by the Federal Bureau of Investigation (Evidence Response Teams, Field Disaster Identification), the Florida Department of Law Enforcement (Evidence Submission Guidelines), and the District 4, State of Florida Medical Examiner's Office.

FINGERPRINT EQUIPMENT

Brushes

- Camel hair (2)
- Fiberglass (3)
- Magnetic wand
- Wide magnetic wand

Powders

- Black (regular and magna)
- Redwop lift
- Silver (regular and magna)

Tape
(must be compatible with powder and cards)

- 2 inches wide
- 4 inches wide
- Rubber tape

Lift Cards
(must be compatible with powder and tape)

- Black
- White
- Regular size and 8 x 12 inches in both colors

Miscellaneous

- Complete cyanoacrylate kit
- Fingerprint cards
- Fingerprint data cards
- Fingerprint ink
- Iodide fuming kit

- Magnifying glass
- Ninhydrin spray
- Silicone
- Transparency sheets

CASTING EQUIPMENT

- Dental powder (2 gallons)
- Dupli-cast
- Identification tags with string
- Metal retaining ring
- Mikrosil rubber
- Mixing bowl (2 sizes)
- Modeling clay (for dam)
- Plaster of paris (5 pounds)

- Plastic bags
- Plastic weigh boats
- Rubber spatula
- Reinforcement mesh
- Silicone casting material
- Snow Wax Spray (for impressions in snow)
- Wooden tongue depressors

PHOTOGRAHIC EQUIPMENT

Cameras

- 35mm with adjustable controls
- 2 1/4 with adjustable controls or larger format
- Extra batteries for cameras

Lens

- Normal
- Macro (capable of 1:1 ratio)
- Telephoto
- Wide angle (28mm maximum)

Film

- Color
- Black and white
- Adequate supply for both formats

Flash

- Batteries
- Compatible strobes for cameras
- PC cord (6–10 feet)
- Power pack for flash

Tripod

- Adjustable legs and height
- Single pod

Measuring Devices

- Disposable rulers

Miscellaneous

- Batteries for camera (extra)
- Blackboard
- Camera carrying cases
- Lens brush and lens tissue
- Photo flood light
- Polaroid w/film or digital camera
- Shutter release cable

Filters

- 80b filter
- Orange filter
- Polarizing

EVIDENCE-PACKAGING SUPPLIES

- Cardboard boxes (assorted)
- Envelopes
- Evidence labels
- Evidence tape
- Glass vials (assorted sizes)
- Manila folders
- Marking pen

- Plastic boxes (assorted sizes)
- Pillboxes (folding)
- Plastic jugs (assorted sizes)
- Plastic Zip-Lock bags
- Stapler
- String tags
- Test tubes with stoppers

- Metal cans (assorted sizes)
- Paper bags (assorted sizes)
- Paper for pharmacy folds
- Twine (heavy)
- Wrapping paper (brown)

BLOOD COLLECTION SUPPLIES

- Disposable scalpel blades
- Distilled water
- Glass microscope plates
- Scalpel
- Small scissors
- Sterilized cloth squares
- Sterilized thread
- Tweezers

DECEASED PRINT KIT

- 2-inch roller
- 4-inch roller
- Black ink
- Finger strips
- Ink remover
- Plain paper
- Porelon pad
- Tissue builder

HAND TOOLS

- Adjustable wrench
- Allen wrench set
- Assorted pliers
- Assorted screwdrivers
- Automobile door handle remover
- Bolt cutters
- Claw hammer
- Drill
- Drywall knives
- Extension cord (heavy duty)
- Glass cutter
- Hacksaw
- Hand ax/hatchet
- Keyhole saw (extra blades)
- Metal cutters
- Needle-nose pliers
- Pipe wrench
- Pocket knife
- Pry bar
- Putty knife
- Rubber mallet
- Shovels
- Sifters
- Slim Jim
- Socket set (metric and standard)
- Vise-Grips
- Wood chisels
- Wire cutters

Measuring Devices

- 26-foot steel tape
- 100-foot tape

PROTECTIVE CLOTHING AND BIOHAZARD KIT

- Cut-resistant gloves
- Disposable biohazards waste bag (trash)
- Disposable coveralls
- Disposable face mask/shield
- Disposable footwear protectors (booties)
- Disposable gown/apron
- Disposable latex gloves

    Regular latex

    Heavy-duty latex (dishwashing style)

- Extended arm-length covered sleeves
- Foul-weather gear
- Hair covers
- Goggles
- Nuisance odor masks
- Particle masks
- Reflective vest
- Rubber boots
- Steel-toed boots

OFFICE SUPPLIES

- 45-degree triangle
- 30-60-degree triangle
- Ballpoint pens
- Clipboards
- Compass (magnetic)
- Drawing compass
- Graph ruled (1/4 inch) pad
- Grease pencil markers
- Markers (permanent)

- Notebook paper
- Paper clips
- Pencils (#2 lead)
- Protractor
- Rubber bands (assorted sizes)
- Scotch tape with dispenser
- Stapler
- Staples
- Thumbtacks

MISCELLANEOUS EQUIPMENT

- 12-foot steel rule
- 100-foot nylon rope
- 100-foot electrical cord
- Cellophane tape and dispenser
- Chalk and crayons
- Cheesecloth
- Clear bookbinding tape

- Magnet (large)
- Magnifying glass
- Metal detector
- Metal scribe
- Numbered cones
- Nylon brush
- Paper towels

- Clipboard
- Colored goggles for ALS (various)
- Compass
- Cotton balls
- Cotton swabs (plastic stem)
- Distilled water
- Extra evidence tape
- Extra staples and stapler
- Eye droppers
- Filter paper
- First-aid kit
- Flags
- Flashlights and spare batteries
- Flex-claw pick-up
- Flex mirror with handle
- Forceps (large and small)
- Generator
- Graph paper
- Gunshot residue kit
- Insect repellent
- Lights (night scenes)

- Pinking shears
- Pipettes and pipette bulbs (box)
- Police seals
- Portable laser or ALS
- Protective eyewear
- Scribes
- Sheets (unused, white cotton)
- Sifting screens
- Shower curtain hooks
- Scissors
- Signs: "Do Not Enter"
- Spatula
- Static lifter
- Tongs
- Tongue depressors (for mixing)
- Tweezers
- Ultraviolet light (low and high wavelength)
- Vacuum cleaner with filters
- Writing and marking pens
- Writing paper and report forms

CHAPTER 8: ELECTRONIC EVIDENCE

CONSIDERATIONS

1)   Just as the computer and other electronic equipment serve an ever-increasing presence in everyday life, so too has that same electronic equipment become much more involved in death investigation. In addition to individuals' recording videotaped suicide messages or leaving suicide notes on their computers, investigators use these same devices for investigative purposes.

    a) ATM transactions not only provide investigators with a photograph of an individual who has just used a homicide victim's bank card moments after the murder, but other, seemingly unrelated, transactions adjacent to a crime scene's location may also provide investigators with street-scene activities.

        i) The increasingly popular surveillance camera not only provides investigators with footage of perpetrators, it can also capture crimes or criminals within the scope and direction of the constant surveillance provided by the camera.

        ii) The video camera can also provide evidence for what the camera did not record. Alibis can soon crumble when a suspect is confronted by a video recording of an area he claimed he had been in (or had not been in), not knowing a video camera had recorded all activities.

    b) Similar to video electronic equipment, a computer may possess not only information concerning the details of a crime, but also incredibly important information concerning the activities of a subject.

        i) A mother may claim to have been watching her child very closely when the child disappeared for "just a couple of minutes." When the child is finally found at the bottom of a backyard pool, computer examination may show Internet log-in times and e-mail messages sent, received, or opened at times that very much contradict the "couple of minutes" scenario supplied by the mother.

    c) Cellular telephones not only supply investigators with the contacts and associates of a subject, as well as the time of incoming or outgoing cell-phone calls, but it may also be important in determining where the calls may have originated. As the cellular signal travels, it passes through a system of communication towers. Investigators may be able to use his information to not only disprove a suspect's alibi but to place him in the vicinity when a crime occurred.

COMPUTER EVIDENCE

(Recommendations by the International Association of Chiefs of Police and the United States Secret Service.)

1)   Preserve area for potential fingerprints.
2)   Immediately restrict access to computers.

    a) Isolate from phone lines because data on the computer can be accessed remotely.

3)   Secure the computer as evidence.

    a) If computer is "off," do not turn "on."

    b) If computer is "on":

        i) Stand-alone computer (not linked to a network)

            (1) Photograph screen.

            (2) Disconnect all power sources; unplug from the wall and the back of the computer.

            (3) Place evidence tape over each drive slot.

            (4) Photograph or diagram the back of the computer, showing the components with observed connections.

(5) Label all connectors or cable ends to allow for reassembly.

(6) If transport is required, package components as fragile cargo.

(a) Keep unit away from all magnets, radio transmitters, and any other environment that may cause damage to the computer or its components.

ii) Network computers

(1) Consult with an electronic specialist.

(a) Pulling the plug could severely damage the system, disrupt legitimate business, or create agency liability.

WIRELESS TELEPHONES

1) How a cellular telephone works

a) As a person uses a cell phone, it is able to work because the telephone signal travels via towers placed strategically through an area. As the user moves from one area of blanket coverage to another, the signal is directed to the closest tower.

b) A cell phone not only contains a telephone number for the particular cell phone, a network entity identifier (NEI), it also contains an equipment identifying number (EIN).

c) When a cell-phone call is placed, the cellular system verifies the NEI and EIN as it verifies and connects the call.

2) Potential evidence includes:

a) Numbers called

b) Numbers stored for speed dial

c) Caller ID for incoming calls

d) Phone or pager numbers

e) Names and addresses of associates

f) Personal identification numbers (PIN)

g) Voice mail access number

h) Voice mail password

i) Debit card numbers

j) Calling card numbers

k) E-mail and Internet access information

3) Cellular intercept potential

a) There are several items that enable law enforcement and other intelligence agencies to use technology in intercepting and locating signals, as well as for other investigative tasks. Because of the sensitive nature of this technology and the ever-changing technological aspects that quickly outdate any written work on this subject material, I won't elaborate any further on this. Legal inquiries into this technology should be directed to the intelligence analysts of the involved agency or the security chiefs of the particular phone company.

4) On-off rule:

a) If the device is "on," do not turn it "off."

i) Turning it "off" could activate the lockout feature.

ii) Write down all information on display, and photograph it if possible.

iii) Power down prior to transport.

(1) Take any power supply cords that may be present.

5) If the device is "off," leave it "off."

a) Turning it "on" could alter available evidence.

b) Upon seizure, take the device to a forensic examiner as soon as possible. If a forensic examiner is not available, consider using a local service representative for the device.

    i) If an expert is not available, use a different telephone, and contact 1-800-LAWBUST.

        (1) This is a 24-hour, 7-day-a-week service provided by the cellular telephone industry.

c) Make every effort to locate any instruction manuals pertaining to the device.

ELECTRONIC PAGING DEVICES

1)   Potential evidence

    a) Numeric pagers

        i) Receive only numeric digits

            (1) Can be used to communicate numbers and code

    b) Alphanumeric pagers

        i) Receive numbers and letters

            (1) Can receive full text messages

    c) Voice pagers

        i) Transmit voice communications

        ii) Some models with alphanumeric capabilities

    d) Two-way pagers

        i) Contain incoming and outgoing messages

2)   Legal considerations

    a) Once pager is no longer in proximity to suspect, turn it off.

        i) Continued access to electronic communications over a pager without proper authorization may be construed as unlawful interception of electronic communication.

FACSIMILE MACHINES

1)   Potential sources of evidence

    a) Speed-dial lists identifying associates, family members, etc.

    b) Stored faxes including incoming and outgoing

    c) Fax transmission logs, including incoming and outgoing

    d) Header line of the fax

    e) Clock setting for the fax

2)   Seizing considerations

    a) If fax machine is found "on," powering down may cause loss of last number dialed or stored faxes.

    b) Identify and record the telephone line number fax is plugged into.

        i) The header line for the fax should be the same as the phone line. The user usually sets the header line.

    c) All manuals should be seized with the equipment.

CALLER ID DEVICES

1)   Potential sources of evidence

    a) Telephone and subscriber information, as well as date and time, from incoming telephone calls

2) Seizing considerations
    a) Interruption of the power supply to the device may cause loss of damage if not protected by an internal battery backup source.
    b) Document all stored data prior to seizure or loss of data may occur.

MISSED-CALL REDIAL

1) Potential source of information
    a) All death scenes containing a telephone should be examined for the last number dialed or the missed-call redial.
        i) The missed-call redial telephone number will appear on the phone bill.

OTHER PHONE COMPANY SERVICES

1) There is no national standard for phone company services any longer. This came about with the forced breakup of the telephone company monopolies. As a result, a phone company has a local and a long-distance provider.
    a) Local provider
        i) If a customer pays a flat rate for local telephone service, the phone company keeps no record of the local call.
    b) Long-distance provider
        i) May be entirely different from the local provider; that company and not the local provider keeps the toll records.
    c) Calling card services
        i) If the customer uses a calling card to place long-distance calls, these records may be separate from those of the other two providers.

2) It is important to identify all the service providers that may have the subject as their customer. Subpoena information must be directed at the particular service provider.

3) Another problem created by the multiple phone company service providers in any particular area involves the phone number of the subject itself. It used to be that a customer had an area code that identified the area in which the phone service exists, the next three digits identified the phone company, and the last four digits identified the customer's account number. Currently, if a customer leaves that particular phone company, he can still keep his original phone number.

4) Work at learning the particular operations of the phone company providing the majority of local telephone service involving the particular jurisdiction of your agency or department.
    a) Get to know the security chief of the local phone company. He will be an excellent source in advising what can and can't be obtained for a particular investigation.
    b) The National Technical Investigators Association (NATIA) lin Falls Church, Virginia, is a national association of sworn law enforcement personnel, whose job responsibilities include electronic issues, including telephone operation.

SMART CARDS

1) What is a smart card?
    a) Identical in size and feel to credit cards, smart cards store information on an integrated microprocessor chip located in the body of the card.
        i) These chips hold a variety of information, from stored (monetary) value used for retail

and vending machines to secure information and applications for such higher end operations as medical/health care records. New information or applications can be added depending on the chip's capabilities.

ii) Contact smart cards must be inserted into a smart card reader. These cards have a contact plate on the face, which makes an electrical connector for reads and writes to and from the chip when inserted into the reader.

iii) Contactless smart cards have an antenna coil, as well as a chip embedded in the card. The internal antenna allows for communication and power with a receiving antenna at the transaction point to transfer information. Close proximity is required for such transactions, which can decrease transaction time while increasing convenience.

iv) A combination card functions as both a contact and contactless smart card.

2)   Uses of a smart card
         a) Point-of-sale transaction
         b) Direct exchange of value between cardholders
         c) Exchange of value over the Internet
         d) ATM capabilities
         e) Storage of other data and files similar to a computer.

3)   Smart card technology is used in some cellular phones and may be found in or with cellular devices.

TRACING AN INTERNET E-MAIL

1) Return path:	leliopul@ncis.navy.mil>
2) Received from:	le03021980.ne.uf (4.1/SMI-4.1) id ZZ081681; Wed, 13 Feb 02 10:22pm EST
3) Received from:	localhost by lm21790.lme.stanton (4.1/SMI-4.1) id JK81681; Wed, 13 Feb 02 10:22 pm EST
4) Message ID:	<111524GE13049@in3224.cc.gizu>
5) From:	Eliopulos, Louis <leliopul@ncis.navy.mil>
6) Sent:	Wednesday, February 13, 2002, 10:22 P.M.
7) To:	Nick Eliopulos <nick@nite.COM>
8) Cc:	Lindsay Eliopulos <lin@vravy.COM>
9) Bcc:	Jason Eliopulos <birdbrain@Os.COM>

Line 1:	Tells other computers the originator of the message and where to send error messages.
Lines 2 and 3:	Show the route the message took from when it was sent to when it was delivered. Each computer receiving this message adds a received field with its complete address and time stamp. This helps in tracking delivery problems.
Line 4:	This is the message ID, a unique identifier for this particular message. This ID is logged and can be traced through computers on the message route if there is a need to track the mail.
Line 5:	Shows the name and e-mail address of the message originator (sender).
Line 6:	Shows the date and time when the message was sent.
Line 7	Shows the name and e-mail address of the primary recipient.
Line 8	Lists the names and e-mail addresses of the "courtesy copy" recipient(s) of the message. There may be "Bcc" (blind carbon copy) recipients as well. These "Bcc" recipients get copies of messages, but their names and addresses are not displayed in the header.

Keep in mind that the investigative significance of e-mails may involve the date and time they may have been sent, as well as e-mails that were *not* sent. For example, let's take a missing person case, where the investigative significance of e-mail can be very important. E-mail received or sent by the missing person will alert investigators to current friends and possible acquaintances of the missing person. However, if the missing person had been receiving daily e-mails from a certain party and those e-mails stop when the victim disappears, that second party may have just alerted investigators that he may have some knowledge about the disappearance.

POSTAL MAIL COVER

1) There are mail services requesting that certain envelopes be photocopied. This action is formally known as a "mail cover."
    a) The main principle is that the outside of envelopes is in the public domain and therefore not subject to privacy protection.

2) The point of contact for any request for a mail cover must be made through the U.S. Postal Inspection Service.

3) A mail cover provides a written record of all data appearing on the outside of any class of mail to obtain information for:
    a) Protecting national security
    b) Locating a fugitive
    c) Obtaining evidence of the commission or attempted commission of a crime punishable by more than one year in prison. A mail cover may not be used in noncriminal investigations, except in those cases involving a civil forfeiture of assets related to violations of criminal laws.

CHAPTER 9: BODY-DUMP SITES

CONSIDERATIONS

1) A body-dump site is an area containing a homicide victim lying above ground, where it is apparent that the victim was not killed at the site but brought there after the homicide.

2) Because the decedent was transported to the dump site after death, the relationship between the body and the area is somewhat less important than the original crime scene or the area of the vehicle used in transporting the remains.

3) What becomes critical in these types of cases is locating and identifying evidence that may link the body with the original scene or the transporting vehicle in the hopes that these features will lead to the identification and prosecution of the perpetrator.

4) If the decedent is a skeleton or badly decomposed, the pathologist may consider consulting with a forensic anthropologist before conducting an autopsy. The significance of finding knife marks, for example, on the bone under microscopic examination may be markedly reduced by the use of a scalpel in that area by the pathologist during the autopsy examination.

PRIMARY FOCUS OF INVESTIGATION

1) Identification of the decedent

2) Cause of death

3) Manner of death

4) Developing the time frame of death

NOTIFICATION

1)   Request that the medical examiner pathologist visit the scene of the recovered remains.

2)   Full crime lab and major case scene should be implemented.

SCENE PHOTOGRAPHS

1)   If homicide is suspected as the manner of death, regular crime-scene photographs should be taken.

2)   Photograph the body from a distance, showing the body's relationship to the area in a 360-degree coverage.

3)   Photograph the body in relation to the surrounding vegetation.

4)   Photograph the vegetation growing around and through the body.

5)   Take photographs of leaves, pine needles, etc., that are covering the body.

6)   After the body has been removed, take photographs of the vegetation and area under the body; include insect activity.

7)   Take individual photographs of each piece of clothing, jewelry, or evidence found on the body or at the scene.

8)   Photograph any items used to cover the remains, especially those that appear not to have occurred through natural means.

9)   Photograph insect activities in detail.
      a) If insect activity appears to be inconsistent with normal decomposition factors, attempt to brush away activity and photograph underlying surface of tissue. Photograph with and without a scale present.

10)   Take close-up photographs of the decedent.
      a) Detail clothing worn and its condition.
      b) Detail obvious injuries to the decedent.
      c) Photograph any indications of the use of restraints, including marks that may have been made by a previously removed restraint.

11)   Photograph items indicative of a struggle.
      a) Photograph torn clothing and missing buttons.
      b) Photograph such personal belongings as the contents of a purse that may have been strewn throughout the area.

SCENE INVESTIGATION

1)   Immediately identify the perimeter of the body-dumping site. Initially access to this area should be restricted to evidence technician.

2)   Determine how the body may have been brought to the site.

        a) Look for tire marks.

        b) Look for footprints.

        c) Was the body carried?

                i) Is the body wrapped in some type of material that will facilitate carrying the remains?

                ii) Are there drag marks leading to the body?

                iii) Is the clothing of the body bunched, disheveled, or dislodged?

3)   Estimate the time frame since placement of the body.

        a) Note foliage over body.

        b) Note plant growth under, around, and through the body.

        c) Note the presence or absence of odor associated with decomposing remains.

        d) Note insect activity.

        e) Note animal activity.

        f) Note the condition of the clothing found on or around the remains.

4)   Check the body for marks indicative of a ligature that may have been removed.

5)   Follow the procedures indicated in Chapter 11.

6)   Check the body for any possible areas of bite marks. If present, follow the bite mark protocols outlined in Chapter 68.

BODY TRANSPORT FROM THE SCENE

1)   Have the evidence technicians collect any obvious foreign material (usually hair and fiber) that may be lost in transport.

2)   Bag (paper) hands of the decedent.

3)   Carefully wrap the body in a clean sheet. Transport the remains to the autopsy facility.

BODY PROCESSING AT THE MEDICAL EXAMINER'S OFFICE

1)   At the medical examiner's office (MEO), the body should be checked for semen stains and additional fibers with ultraviolet (UV) light or ALS.

2)   Consider checking the body for fingerprints by ALS.

3)   Collect the sheet (fold sheet to preserve) used to transport the body to the autopsy facility.

        a) If body is covered with dirt and debris from the scene, brush the material off the body and onto the sheet.

4)   Collect the bags used to cover the decedent's hands during transport to the MEO.

5)   Pull head hair standards.

6)   Collect pulled and combed pubic hair.

7)   Collect left- and right-hand fingernail scrapings.

8)   Collect oral, anal, and vaginal swabbings on females.

9)   Collect oral and anal swabbings on males. Consider collecting penis swabbing for the presence of saliva.

10)   Collect enough blood required to run all tests.

11)   Collect major case prints on the decedent.

12)   If a firearm is involved, perform neutron activation swabbing of the decedent's hands. Collect the projectile.

13)   Collect and separately bag any clothing recovered.

FOLLOW-UP INVESTIGATION

1)   Continue efforts to identify the decedent.

CHAPTER 10: BURIED-BODY CASES

Lord, Grant Me the Serenity
To Accept the Things
I Cannot Change,
The Courage to Change
The Things I Can
And the Wisdom
To Hide the Bodies
Of Those People
I Had to Kill Because
They Pissed Me Off.
—Anonymous

CONSIDERATIONS

1) A shallow or deep burial may be involved.

2) Processing should only take place under optimal lighting and weather conditions.
   a) Unless other considerations are appropriate, processing should begin in the daylight hours when enough time exists for the proper processing of the area and the appropriate participants are present.
   b) Consider erecting a tent to assist participants during the processing in inclement weather.

3) Investigation is usually concentrated in an area the investigator has been led to by a participant of the burial or by a person who has discovered something suspicious. In those cases in which only the general area is known, the investigator is at a distinct disadvantage. The smaller the area to be searched, the better the chances are for a successful recovery. In those cases in which the exact area is not known, the investigator should consider the following:
   a) Use ground radar enhancement.
   b) Use aerial infrared photography.
   c) Check the appearance of a small area in which the vegetation is absent or the vegetation growth is inconsistent with other vegetation in the area.
      i) Vegetation will be absent in recent burials because digging destroys the roots.
      ii) An overall dry area of vegetation may contain a small area of rich, green vegetation as a result of the added nutrients a decomposing body adds to the soil.
      iii) Vegetation may be collected and placed over the grave area. Small piles of dead shrubs, branches, and leaves over a particular area may signal a hidden grave.
   d) Examine the terrain for sunken areas. The soil around the buried body will eventually fill in completely around the body and be compacted as rainwater filters through the soil. Grave areas initially level with the surrounding area will eventually begin to sink, taking on the appearance of a depression and ultimately assume the width and length of the original excavation.
   e) In recent burials, a pile of dirt may be visible. This dirt pile collects because the body has displaced the dirt.
      i) In an effort to conceal this displaced dirt, the digger may feel compelled to hide the grave and, therefore, prefer not to form a mound with the "extra" dirt. This dirt may be scattered throughout the site. The investigator should examine the area for a site in which the topsoil appearance (color and texture) is different from that of the surrounding area.

4) Once the area has been tentatively identified, digging into the soil surface should reveal a mixture of soil, not the expected soil present in tiers in an undisturbed area.

5) Never use a sharp-edged instrument near the buried remains.

Buried-body excavation.

PRIMARY FOCUS OF INVESTIGATION

1) Identifying the decedent

2) Developing the cause of death

3) Developing the manner of death

4) Developing the time frame of death through the following:
   a) Examination of the remains
   b) Examination of plant material
   c) Examination of insect activity
   d) Examination of clothing or other materials associated with the death

NOTIFICATION

1) Forensic pathologist

2) Forensic anthropologist

3) Full lab capabilities

SCENE PHOTOGRAPHS

1) Overall area
   a) Consider aerial photography.
   b) Demonstrate remoteness of the area.

2) Show landmark features in relation to the burial site

3) Photograph areas indicative of suspect's efforts and activities while at this site.
   a) Tire impressions
   b) Foot or shoe impressions
   c) Discarded cigarette butts or cigarette packs
   d) Discarded cans, cups, or bottles
   e) Broken branches or disturbed shrubbery
   f) Drag marks
   g) Any other articles possibly left behind
   h) Any possible weapon
   i) Other articles possibly relating to the death
      i) Shell casings

          ii) Spent projectiles
          iii) Articles of clothing
       j) Blood spatter relating to movement or activity on the part of the victim or suspect

4)   Photograph the grave area.
       a) Show the sunken area, soil changes, or other indications of the burial.
       b) Show the overall area prior to and after the removal of the ground debris surrounding this area.
       c) As the exhumation begins, photograph any sign showing the possible tool used by the digger during the original digging.

5)   Photograph the excavation site at various stages of the process.

6)   Photograph any items relating to the incident that you encounter during the exhumation, including jewelry, clothing, towels, buttons, and shell casings.

7)   Photograph the decedent from a distance and closeup, going around the body in 360-degree coverage.

8)   Photograph any items that may have been used to transport or cover the remains.

9)   Photograph the body in relation to the surrounding vegetation.
       a) Take photographs of the vegetation, including root structure, growing around and through the body.
       b) After the body has been removed, photograph the type and condition of vegetation under the body.

10)   Photograph insect activity in detail.
       a) If any insect activity appears to be inconsistent with known decomposition factors, attempt to brush away the activity and photograph underlying surface tissue with and without a scale present. (Be sure to include anatomical landmarks in the photograph.)

11)   Photograph the decedent.
       a) Photographs should show the relationship between the decedent the depth of the hole. Use scales and directional indicator.
       b) Take close-up photographs of the decedent's remains on a section-to-section basis. Be sure to use anatomical references in each photograph.
       c) Photograph clothing. Detail condition.
       d) Photograph obvious injuries involving the remains.
       e) Photograph any indication of restraints, including marks that may be present and may have been produced by a previously removed restraint.
       f) Photographs any signs that may tend to be indicative of a struggle.
       i) Photograph torn clothing, missing buttons, drag mark abrasions, or defense-type wounds on the decedent's hands and arms.

12)   After the digging has concluded and the remains have been removed, photograph the hole.
       a) Photographs should be taken with and without measuring scales present. The scales help to identify the width and depth of the hole. A directional arrow should be placed in the photograph indicating north.

SCENE INVESTIGATION

1)   Determine the surface area involved. Clear the area of surface debris (e.g., leaves, pine needles, underbrush, branches).

2) Dig very carefully. Never use a bladed tool in close proximity to the remains.
    a) Use a flat-bladed spade or hand trowel.
    b) Preserve the area of the original grave.
        i) Depending on the type of soil involved, you may be able to see tool marks from the original instrument used in digging the site, which could lead to the identification of the instrument.

3) The soil should be removed evenly in 6-inch sections. All dirt removed from the site should be sifted through a screen.

4) Any item recovered in the exhumation should be photographed and handled in anticipation of processing for fingerprints.

5) Upon reaching the remains, exercise extreme caution when removing the dirt surrounding the body. The dirt should be removed in such a manner that eventually the body will lie atop the soil only.
    a) Be careful of any item used to wrap the remains or any object in which the remains were placed. Fingerprints can still be recovered from such items as plastic bags, wooden or cardboard boxes, etc.
    b) Place the body in a clean white sheet.

6) After the body has been removed, do the following:
    a) Dig and sift the dirt for several more inches.
    b) Use a metal detector if gunshot wounds are suspected or cannot be eliminated as a potential cause of death.

BODY TRANSPORT FROM SCENE

1) Carefully wrap the body in a clean sheet. Transport to the MEO.
    a) If recovery involves skeletal remains, consider placing the remains in a cardboard box for transfer.

BODY PROCESSING AT THE MEO

1) If possible, collect major case prints.

2) Collect the body transport sheet (fold sheet inward for preservation) used to transport the remains.
    a) If a body is covered with dirt and debris from the scene, brush the material off the body and onto the sheet before collecting the sheet.

3) Collect head hair standards.

4) Collect pubic hair standards.

5) Collect a tube of blood if possible. If blood is not available, collect bone marrow.

6) If a firearm may be involved, collect all projectiles.

7) Collect and separately bag all clothing items.
    a) If identification is a consideration, each piece of clothing should be individually searched for pocketed items, laundry, or other identifying marks, clothing manufacturer, color, and size.

i) Clothing can be submitted for laboratory analysis to determine the time frame involved in the breakdown of fabric fibers. Natural fibers breakdown much more quickly than synthetic fibers.

FOLLOW-UP INVESTIGATION

1)   Continue efforts to identify decedent.

2)   If death is by homicide, follow procedures indicative of the motive involved.

LOOKING FOR BURIED BODIES

Necro Search
Necro Search is an organization currently comprising 38 professionals from various disciplines or fields whose objective is to develop and refine detection techniques for clandestine graves. These experts meet as a group to review a case, which is then assigned to an officer to work. Necro Search does not charge for its services, but it does require the involved agency to pay for any expenses associated with working the case.

CONSIDERATIONS

1)   Three considerations that may affect the outdoor crime scene:
          a) Vegetation
          b) Insects (entomology)
          c) Scavengers

2)   As in other outdoor scenes, when processing this type of scene it is a good idea to have the investigators and all other visitors to the scene place a strip of duct tape on the bottom of each shoe to identify and distinguish any shoe prints of recent origin.

3)   Do not use heavy machinery to search for remains because it will destroy any spatial relationship of that potential scene.
          a) Ground-penetrating radar is a nonintrusive alternative.

4)   The investigative techniques associated with recovering remains from an outdoor setting should proceed from the least destructive to the most intrusive. They include the following:
          a) Aerial photography
                i) It is ideal in every case to have aerial photography of the suspected area.
                ii) There are two companies in the United States that put up satellites with 1-meter resolution capabilities (able to recognize an object at 1 meter).
                iii) When dealing with an aerial photograph, there are two considerations:
                        (1) Pattern recognition
                        (2) Resolution (detail)
                iv) If you are dealing with aerial photographs, note that these photographs can only be enlarged four times without causing the photographs to become fuzzy and therefore jeopardizing the ability to analyze the photographs.
                v) In aerial photography it should be understood that as a plane travels it is continuously taking photographs. This causes an overlap of photographs involving a factor of approximately 60 percent.
                        (1) The investigator working the case and seeking analysis should attempt to acquire all of the photographs from the involved area.

(2) The overlapping photographs can provide the analyst with what basically translates into a stereoscopic and three-dimensional image of the involved area when viewed with a specialized pair of stereoscopic glasses.

vi) If photographs of the involved area are shot in anticipation of having an analytical review, do not take them from a perpendicular perspective.

    (1) The camera should be held at a slight angle, not perpendicular when taking the aerial photograph. This is done for two reasons:

        (a) The analyst can see the soil mark as a pattern.

        (b) Shadow marks and highlights are subject to analysis.

            (i) Use shadows.

                1. Photographs are better suited for interpretation when shadows are created by the natural lighting condition. High noon is not the best time for shadow development.
Early in the morning and late in the afternoon are the best times (oblique lighting conditions) for taking photographs where shadows and textures are highlighted.

vii) Current experimentation with model airplanes (drones) with an 8-foot wing span, a stall speed of 8 miles per hour, and a camera has produced excellent aerial photographs for later analysis.

    (1) This technique is relatively inexpensive and may also be beneficial in those cases where permission from property owners may be difficult to obtain because they cannot be found or or various other reasons.

    (2) This technique has proven beneficial for flying over and assessing mass-disaster sites.

viii) There are numerous secondary sources of aerial photographs, limited only by the imagination of the investigator. The best possible source is the tax assessor's office. Most assessors take photographs of tax-assessed properties every 3 years. This not only affords the investigator with an aerial photograph of the involved area, but it can also be used to establish the investigation with a time line of the involved area. Government sources of photographs to check include (but should not be limited to):

    (1) U.S. Geological Survey

    (2) Soil Conservation Service

    (3) Forestry Service

    (4) Bureau of Land Management

    (5) Bureau of Reclamation

    (6) Bureau of Mines

    (7) National Park Service

ix) Secondary sources of aerial photographs should include (but not be limited to):

    (1) Tax assessor's office

        (a) This is the best possible source, since many tax assessor's offices take aerial photographs every 3 years. For comparison basis, the dated photographs can supply the analyst with a timel ine of photos over the involved area.

    (2) Railroads

    (3) Highway department

    (4) Utility company

    (5) Pipeline companies

    (6) Developers

b) Thermal infrared imagery (FLIR)

    i) Detects sources of heat within subject matter

    ii) Is used as a detection technique to locate clandestine graves

    iii) Analyst must determine which color represents "hot" and which depicts "cold."

    iv) Detection tool capability is this:

        (1) Although skeletal remains do not generate heat, a disturbance in the soil may be detected.

            (a) FLIR can detect .20°C in temperature change in the disturbed soil.

c) Geophysics

    i) Geophysics uses mathematics, geology, and physics to study the interior of the earth without disturbing it.

    ii) The premise in searching for a grave involves an understanding the disturbance a soil undergoes in association with digging and backfilling a hole.

        (1) The soil placed back into a hole is never returned to the same density as before the hole was dug. The replaced soil is much looser, which affects the way electricity travels through the ground.

    iii) Local utilities should be consulted before conducting any search to eliminate the possibility of uncovering utility-related items.

    iv) The person conducting the search should be dressed as "clean" as possible. The searcher should not wear steel-toed shoes, wire rimmed glasses, etc.

    v) The following tools may be used by a geophysicist:

        (1) Metal detectors

            (a) A geologist attempts to measure contrasts. For example, if a gun is placed in the sand, there is a contrast between the soil and the handgun. If a plastic gun is placed in the same soil, the contrast is not as great. A geologist attempts to analyze the contrast.

Buried-body grave site. As the soil gets packed by rain and the collapse of the decomposing body, the surface area will show a depression where the collapsing occurred. A deeper depression or a secondary depression may occur over the body area itself. Cracks in the soil may allow insects access to the body; cracks may also let scents escape, which may alert a cadaver dog.

(i) The first step is to grid off the area of concern.

(ii) Metal detectors are very rarely used correctly. The circular heads of metal detectors contain two coils. One coil sends signals into the ground; the second coil receives the signal. If a signal is received, it indicates that a different type of material is present.

(iii) Newer detectors (costing $1,000 or more) can discriminate for search items. For example, if someone is looking for a 9mm casing, a 9mm casing is placed up to the metal detector. The detector is then set to look for an item of similar composition.

(iv) Metal detectors only detect ferrous or nonferrous items.
    1. Ferrous metals will rust.
    2. Nonferrous metals will not.

(v) The correct search/sweep pattern to be used with a metal detector is shown here.

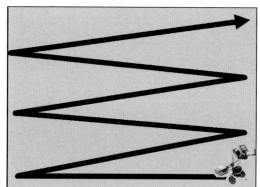

Incorrect sweep pattern.

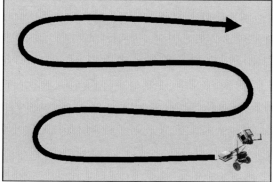

Correct sweep pattern.

(vi) Different detectors use different frequencies. If multiple detectors are used at a scene, these different frequencies may cancel out each other.

(2) Electromagnetic surveying tool

  (a) This is used to look for such larger items as safes and cars (ferrous and nonferrous metals). Depending on the equipment used, the electro-magnetic surveying equipment can search for ferrous and nonferrous metals at a depth of 5 to 18 feet.

(3) Magnetometer

  (a) Searches for iron and steel (ferrous metal).

  (b) Can find a body even if it is not wearing metal because the soil has a magnetic field that has become magnetized over the years. The magnetometer identifies a disruption in the soil that may have occurred when a grave was dug and then refilled.

    (i) This technique, like the others, locates anomalies in the soil, not bodies.

  (c) Workers seaching for pipes and valves usually use magnetometers. Water and utility companies usually have these items.

    (i) A magnetometer is capable of finding a 10-penny nail at a depth of 10 feet.

(4) Ground-penetrating radar (GPR)

        (a) GPR uses an antenna and two coils. It works by sending a magnetic pulse into the ground, which generates a return signal to the unit. These pulses that are sent and returned create a high-resolution, cross-sectional image of the ground.

        (b) Penetration of the signal is greatly influenced by the soil composition. The geophysicist, however, will be looking for disruptions in the layers of the soil.

        (c) GPR can also be used on walls and ceilings because its signal can penetrate concrete.

            (i) Structured concrete is strengthened by reinforcing bar (rebar). If the rebar rods are closer than 4 inches, the GPR will have trouble penetrating the concrete.

            (ii) Checking with the agency responsible for issuing building permits should reveal the "as built" plans. These records should describe the slab structure.

        (d) GPR can work through fresh water, but not saltwater, for distances up to 30 feet.

            (i) It can be used in conjunction with a fish finder to map the bottom of a lake.

            (ii) Another tool to be used in either salt or fresh water is the Side-Scan Sonar.

                1. This is typically employed by dragging the unit behind a boat.

                2. It is fairly useful for finding a car underwater. It is not very useful for locating a gun.

                3. The side-scan sonar requires a very good operator. The resolution can look similar to a black and white photograph.

    vi) A geologist may be able to prepare an idealized soil profile by interpreting the dark-colored surface of the soil characterized by decomposing organic material.

        (1) As the criminal digs into the earth, he begins disturbing the soil. The disturbance of the soil may indicate a suspicious area where a body may have been buried.

    vii) Probes may be employed to search for possible buried remains.

        (1) Do not use a probe with a sharpened end. Probes are available with a bulb-style end.

d) Botany

    i) A forensic botanist is used for analysis.

        (1) Vegetation may be disturbed or after the digging of the grave.

        (2) Vegetation associated with the grave may appear different from the surrounding area.

e) Entomology

    i) Insects live to eat—especially blowflies. Insects get into the grave system. Insect and larvae collection can provide analysts with a time frame for the death.

f) Cadaver dogs

    i) The olfactory sense in dogs is much more highly sensitive than that of humans. Certain dogs can be trained in locating decomposing remains, skeletal remains, and bodies in water.

g) Scavenger patterns

i) Bird nests, burrow holes, and anthills should all be checked in areas around suspected sites for evidence of the missing remains.

   (1) Fiber-optic cable can be used to search burrowed holes in suspected areas.

h) Test trenching/archeology

   i) Archeological procedures, including the digging of a trench alongside the suspected grave area, may be implemented.

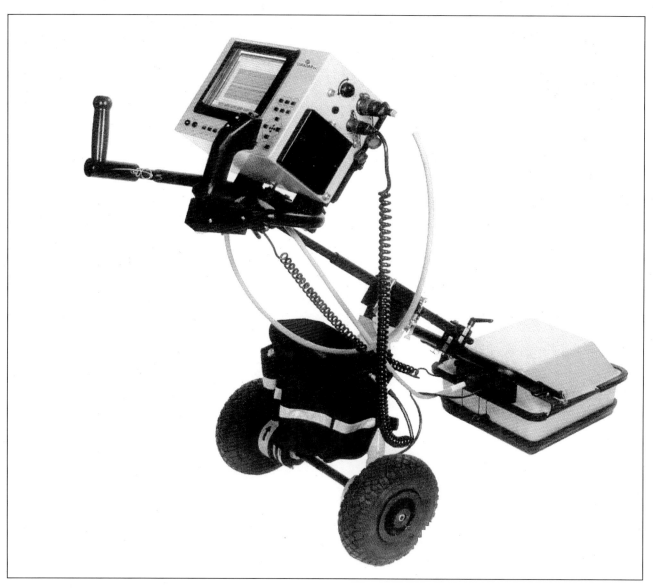

Ground-penetrating radar.

CHAPTER 11: DECOMPOSED REMAINS

CONSIDERATIONS

1)   Decomposition cases involve decedents who who have obviously been dead for some time. Post-mortem changes are in an advanced state and may alter cause-of-death indicators and may cause difficulties in identifying the decedent.

2)   Decomposition follows these stages:
    a) Fresh
        i) Days 1 and 2
        ii) No visible changes in the decedent.
        iii) Flies arrive within minutes and begin depositing instar larvae into dark, moist areas of the head (eyes, nose, and mouth).
        iv) Ants arrive.
            (1) The quantity of maggots may be influenced by the number of ants present. The ants feed on the instar larvae.
        v) Wasps arrive. They feed on the adult flies and exudates present from the remains.
    b) Bloated
        i) Days 2 to 6
        ii) House flies are attracted to the remains.
            (1) House flies lay eggs that hatch in 5 days.
        iii) Ants are still busy and quite obvious in their activities.
        iv) The first area (head) is infested. Maggots begin a second area of infestation, the genital area (particularly the anus).
    c) Decayed
        i) Days 7 to 11
        ii) Insect activity pierces the bloated abdomen, causing it to collapse.
        iii) Diptera pupa present—third instar larval stage.
        iv) Domestic beetles arrive, which feed on the dry skin and cartilage.
        v) Larvae of beetles are present on the 11th day.
        vi) The body weight of the decedent decreases dramatically during the first 10 days.
        vii) Ant activities begin to slow down as they eat the larvae. The more ants, the fewer larvae to eat. Fewer larvae, fewer ants.
    d) Mummified or dry
        i) Days 12 to 25
        ii) Beetles increase in numbers.
    e) Post-decay
        i) Days 10 to 23
        ii) Remains never dry off enough for many kinds of insects to invade. Some insects come in as predators and feed on the larvae.
    f) Remains
        i) Day 26 and after
        ii) Beetles remain up to 50 days
        iii) Pupa will still be present

3)   Irregular decomposition with regard to insect activity may indicate an antemortem injury, exposing blood and underlying tissue. Insects attack wounds immediately.

a) Postmortem damage must be ruled out through careful autopsy examination of the underlying area of bone.

b) Maggots found on the palms of the decedent's hands may indicate defense wounds.

c) Larvae (maggots) along the decedent's arms may indicate a drug abuser.

4) Skeletal remains most often contain the remains of insects that can be useful in identifying the season in which the death may have occurred.

5) Canines will take the head of a decedent and use it as a toy.

a) It is not unusual to find the head of the decedent a distance away from the main body.

b) Striations may be present where the animal has attempted to grip the skull with its teeth. The animal will rotate the skull until it can grip the skull by an orbit or the maxilla. The animal may then take the skull to a nearby area it uses as a windscreen.

(1) Inexperienced investigators may misinterpret the small triangular punctures caused by the animal's canines as the punctures from an ice pick.

6) The decedent's hair may be found in bird nests in nearby trees.

7) Rodents may carry off rings, teeth, bones, bullets, etc., and place them in small holes adjacent to the body.

8) Collecting and noting of vegetation found with the remains can be useful in estimating the time frame of death.

PRIMARY FOCUS OF INVESTIGATION

1) Identification of the decedent

2) Cause and manner of death

3) Developing the time frame of death

NOTIFICATION

1) Consider requesting the pathologist to come to scenes in which the cause or manner of death is not readily apparent.

2) If homicide is suspected as the manner of death, regular homicide notification procedures should be applied.

SCENE PHOTOGRAPHS

1) If homicide is suspected as the manner of death, regular homicide scene photographs should apply.

2) If homicide is not suspected, include the following in the overall photographs taken of the scene:

a) Outdoor scene photographs

i) If the remains are taken from a body of water, identification-type photographs should be taken immediately because the body's appearance, including color, will begin deteriorating rapidly as the remains are removed from the water.

    ii) Photograph the body from a distance, showing the body's relationship to the area in a 360-degree coverage.

    iii) Photograph the body in relationship to the surrounding vegetation.

    iv) If body parts are separated, attempt to photograph each section of body in relation to the main section of the remains.

        (1) Photograph clothing, jewelry, and other evidence found separate from the remains.

        (2) Take individual photographs of each section of the remains.

        (3) Take individual photographs of each piece of clothing, jewelry, or other pieces of evidence found at the scene.

    v) Take photographs of the vegetation growing around and through the body.

    vi) After the body has been removed, take photographs of the vegetation and area under the body, including insect activity.

    vii) Be sure to photograph any items found covering the remains, especially if those items do not appear to have occurred naturally.

    viii) Photograph insect activity in detail.

        (1) If insect activity appears to be inconsistent with normal decomposition factors, attempt to brush away the activity and photograph underlying surface of tissue with and without scale present.

b) Indoor scene photographs

    i) Take overall shots of the premises

    ii) Take photographs showing the condition of the doors and windows.

    iii) Take photographs of items, which may indicate a general time frame (e.g., newspapers collected on the front porch).

    iv) Take photographs of items that may indicate the activities of the decedent prior to death.

    v) Photograph the general condition of the room in which the body is found.

    vi) Photograph any items out of place relative to the decedent or the location in which the decedent is found.

    vii) Photograph any valuables present in relation to the body, which may exclude the possibility of robbery (e.g., an expensive watch on the decedent's wrist).

    viii) Photograph any prescription vials found adjacent to the decedent.

    ix) Photograph any alcohol containers, drugs, or drug paraphernalia that may be relative to the decedent's cause of death.

    x) Take close-up photographs of the decedent.

        (1) Detail clothing worn and condition.

        (2) Detail insect infestation.

SCENE INVESTIGATION

1)   Note the type of area in which the decedent was found.

    a) Why is the decedent here?

    b) How did the decedent get here?

2)   Note the time frame of death as evidenced by the environment (e.g., type of vegetation covering the remains).

3)   Follow the guidelines suggested under the particular type of death the investigators feel may have been involved. If uncertain about a suspected cause of death, treat the death as a homicide. Follow the guidelines for suspected homicide handling.

4)   If outdoors, collect plant specimens.
        a) Place specimens in a paper bag and refrigerate them until such time as they can be delivered to a forensic botanist.

5)   If the decedent is found indoors and is believed to live in the residence, search for the decedent's address book. This may assist in finding next of kin or a dentist, should identification of the decedent become a problem.

ENTOMOLOGY CONSIDERATIONS

1)   Information an entomologist can provide the following to death investigators:
        a) Time since death may be established based on one or more of the following:
            i) Species succession
            ii) Larval weight or length
            iii) Accumulated temperature by degree/hour technique
        b) Postmortem movement of the body may be calculated.
        c) Insect infestation may also supply investigators with circumstances of abuse or sexual assaults.
            i) Clothing, diapers, and wounds of incapacitated victims sometimes contain maggot activity.
        d) DNA from the victim and/or suspect may be collected within the digestive track of blood-feeding insects.
            i) The presence of this DNA may be legally significant in placing the victim and the suspect at a known location within a specified period. In addition, this type of evidence may be used to provide an evidentiary link between the suspect and the victim.
        e) When human tissue and fluids are no longer available for examination, toxicological analysis may be possible on insects that fed on the recovered skeletal remains.

2)   This is collection equipment needed at the death scene.

- Folding insect net
- Thermos of scalding water
- Gloves
- Plastic vials for adult flies, beetles, and other insects
- Killing jar
- Temperature probes
- Trowel
- Zip-Loc baggies
- Alcohol wipes
- Prepared perforated (pin-hole size) baggies with slightly moistened vermiculite, raw animal liver, and cardboard roll (to prevent baggie from collapsing and smashing specimens)
- Forceps
- Data loggers
- Assorted jars
- Ethanol, 75 percent

3)   Collect temperature from the following:
        a) Various locations on the body
        b) Wherever the insects will be collected
        c) Body surface temperature
        d) Outdoor scenes
            i) Soil surface temperature
                (1) Record temperature at scene for 1 to 2 weeks after discovery of the body.
                (2) Place indoor/outdoor, minimum/maximum digital recorder to record temperature 4 feet above the ground.
                (3) Do not place recording device in direct sunlight.
                (4) The equipment should be able to record temperature every 30 minutes to 1 hour.
        e) Indoor scenes
            i) If the scene is indoors, do not open windows or doors until temperature and insect collection have been completed.

4)   Collect living insects.
        a) Collect egg masses.
        b) Collect adult flies and other insects at the scene.
        c) Check soil for pupae and postfeeding larvae.
            i) Check the area immediately under the body once the body has been moved from the scene.
            ii) Also examine the areas 6 feet and 12 feet away from where the head lay.
                (1) Some entomologists recommend that areas from 4, 8, 12, and 16 feet should be examined for migrating pupae and larvae.
        d) Create and place labels inside collection baggies. Include the following:
            i) Insect stage collected (eggs, larvae, and pupae)
            ii) Date, time, and location of insects' collection (example of location: victim's chest)
                (1) Temperature should be taken for every specimen collected.

5) Kill and preserve the following:
        a) One-third to one-half of living fly specimens should be killed and preserved. Use plastic vials for storage.
        b) Keep all pupae alive.
        c) Kill eggs/larvae by placing them in a bowl (coffee-less cup) of scalding water for a few minutes. Transfer specimens to a 75-percent ethanol solution.
            i) 30 to 60 eggs/larvae should be collected; one-third to one-half of the specimens will be killed.
        d) Living larvae should be placed in sample collection bags with raw liver pieces.
            i) Pupae do not need liver.

ENTOMOLOGY SCENE REPORT—SAMPLE SHEET

DEATH SCENE REPORT — ENTOMOLOGICAL

CASE

LOCATION

INCIDENT NUMBER

DATE/ TIME FOUND

DATE/ TIME PROCESSED

VICTIM LAST NAME, FIRST, MIDDLE ☐ Unknown

SEX

DOB/ AGE

HABITAT

URBAN/ SUBURBAN (Check all that apply)
- ☐ Business
- ☐ Residential
- ☐ Industrial
- ☐ Vacant lot
- ☐ Park
- ☐ Parking lot
- ☑ Roadside
- ☐ Yard
- ☐ Other (describe)

RURAL (Check all that apply)
- ☐ Farm/ Ranch land
- ☐ Woodland
- ☐ Grassland
- ☐ Desert
- ☐ Rural residential area
- ☐ Agricultural field
- ☐ Agricultural orchard
- ☐ Deciduous forest
- ☐ Coniferous forest
- ☐ Mixed Coniferous/ Deciduous forest
- ☐ Brush
- ☐ Roadside
- ☐ Pasture
- ☐ Landfill
- ☐ Other (description)

WETLAND (Check all that apply)
- ☐ Freshwater
- ☐ Saltwater
- ☐ Brackish water
- ☐ Lake/ Pond
- ☐ Stream/ River
- ☐ Marsh/ Swamp
- ☐ Irrigation ditch
- ☐ Shoreline/ Beach
- ☐ River bottom
- ☐ Other (describe)

NOTES

SITE

SURFACE
- ☐ Asphalt
- ☐ Concrete
- ☐ Structure/ Bldg floor
- ☐ Grass/ plants
- ☐ Sand
- ☐ Mud
- ☐ Soil/ dirt
- ☐ Leaf litter
- ☐ Rocky
- ☐ Other (describe)

EXPOSURE (Check all that apply)
- ☐ Open area
- ☐ Closed structure
- ☐ Open Structure
- ☐ Closed vehicle
- ☐ Open vehicle
- ☐ Submerged
- ☐ Partially submerged
- ☐ Closed container
- ☐ Open container
- ☐ Buried (describe depth)
- ☐ Other (describe)

DAILY SUNLIGHT
- ☐ Full sun
- ☐ Partial sun
- ☐ Full shade
- ☐ Partial shade
- ☐ Hours of sunlight on body (estimated hours/day)

NOTES

WEATHER

GENERAL WEATHER CONDITIONS
- ☐ Sunny
- ☐ Partly sunny
- ☐ Cloudy
- ☐ Partly cloudy
- ☐ Fog
- ☐ Snow
- ☐ Rain
- ☐ Hail

Date/ Time: _____

ENVIRONMENTAL MEASUREMENTS

Ambient Temperature _____ Date/ Time: _____

Relative Humidity _____ Date/ Time: _____

Water Temperature _____ Date/ Time: _____

NOTES

AGENCY

REPORTING OFFICER

DATE

INCIDENT NUMBER

Death Scene Report — Entomological

AGENCY	OFFICER	DATE

BODY/ REMAINS

BODY POSITION

☐ Prone ☐ Supine ☐ Right side down ☐ Left side down ☐ Sitting ☐ Scattered parts
☐ Other (describe)

BODY COVERING (Check all that apply)

☐ Fully covered ☐ Mostly covered ☐ Partially covered ☐ Nude - No covering
☐ L/sleeve shirt ☐ S/sleeve shirt ☐ Long pants ☐ Short pants ☐ Socks ☐ Shoes/ Boots
☐ Jacket/ Coat ☐ Sweater ☐ Hat ☐ Gloves ☐ Plastic bag ☐ Sheet plastic
☐ Other (description)

STAGE OF DECOMPOSITION

☐ Fresh ☐ Bloat ☐ Decay ☐ Dry ☐ Mummified ☐ Remains
☐ Other (describe)

SUSPECTED TRAUMA (describe)

EVIDENCE OF SCAVENGERS (describe)

TEMPERATURE MEASUREMENTS

Body surface _____ Date/ Time: _____ Location _____

Under body _____ Date/ Time: _____ Location _____

Maggot mass _____ Date/ Time: _____ Location _____

Maggot mass _____ Date/ Time: _____ Location _____

Soil 10 cm deep _____ Date/ Time: _____ Location _____

Soil 20 cm deep _____ Date/ Time: _____ Location _____

NOTES

INSECT ACTIVITY

INSECT ACTIVITY

On the body diagrams to the left, shade or otherwise mark the location(s) of suspected insect activity especially eggs and/or larva. Refer to these locations on the collection sheets. Keep specimens collected from different sites of the body separate.

Check each stage of development believed to be observed on the body/ remains.

☐ Eggs ☐ Larva ☐ Pupae/ Puparia ☐ Adults

NOTES/ OBSERVATIONS

Page 2

CHAPTER 12: TIME FRAME OF DEATH

The death or forensic investigator should record his observations at the scene so that a forensic pathologist can interpret their significance.

IMPORTANT NOTE: Environment, temperature, and moisture affect all deaths. The chart below should be used for *approximation purposes only.*

CONDITION	APPEARANCE

BLOOD

Blood drying (periphery)	30 minutes to 2 hours

POSTMORTEM LIVIDITY

First detectable	Immediate to 2 hours
Full setting	8 to 12 hours

When cardiac activity stops, the hydrostatic pressure of the liquid (blood) causes it to settle and distend into the dependent capillary bed. Livor mortis will not usually develop where there is pressure from clothing or objects.

RIGOR MORTIS

First detectable	1 to 6 hours
Fully developed	6 to 24 hours
Disappears	12 to 36 hours

Muscular relaxation immediately after death is followed by the onset of gradual rigidity as glycogen in the muscle is converted to lactic acid. As the pH in the muscle falls, there is a physical change in the muscle protoplasm. Since this is a chemical process, it is accelerated by heat and decelerated by cold. Illness, temperature, activity before death, and the physical conditions of the area where the body was placed or is found also affect the process. Rigor mortis may be poorly formed in the old or the young. Once someone has broken rigor, it will not reform.

ALGOR MORTIS

A person's metabolism generates heat, which is closely regulated by the body within a fairly narrow range. After death, the heat production ceases, and the body will cool to the approximate ambient temperature.

98.6°F - measured rectal temperature ÷ 1.5 = hours since death

STAGES OF POSTMORTEM DECOMPOSITION

Blue-green discoloration of skin	24 hours
Right and left area of abdomen	36 hours
Entire abdomen	
Bloating	36 to 48 hours
Marbling	2 to 3 days
Green-black discoloration in the blood vessel distribution as a result of the hemolyzed blood reacting with hydrogen sulfide.	
Skin blistering	3 days
Entire body decomposition	60–72 hours
Purging	4 to 5 days
Skin slippage (epidermolysis)	4 to 7 days
Hair and nails loosen and shed. "Glove" formation of hands and feet.	
Adipocere (saponification)	Months
(Adipocere is the prolonged exposure of the body to moisture.)	
Mummification	Weeks to years
Drying precedes or interrupts decomposition	
Skeletonization	Weeks to years
Absence of smell from bones	More than 1 year

Weathering of bones depends on whether the body is buried, climate, moisture, elevation, terrain, protection, and insect and animal activity.

EYEBALL CHANGES

CONDITION	APPEARANCE
Cornea drying (open eyelids)	Minutes
Cornea drying (closed eyelids)	Several hours
Schleral discoloration (tache noire)	Minutes to several hours
Corneal cloudiness (open eyelids)	Less than 2 hours
Corneal cloudiness (closed eyelids)	12 to 24 hours
Exophthalmoses (bulging)	With gas formation
Eyeball collapse	More than 24 hours

All depend on lid position, temperature, humidity, and air currents.

STOMACH CONTENTS

SIZE OF MEAL	TIME IN STOMACH
Light-size meal	1 1/2 to 2 hours
Medium-size meal	3 to 4 hours
Heavy-size meal	4 to 6 hours

NOTE: Processing of the stomach contents depends on many factors, including the emotional state of the decedent prior to death, whether the subject had consumed alcohol with the meal, and whether the subject suffered from digestive disorders.

Liquids are processed faster than semisolids, which are processed faster than solids.

CHAPTER 13: BLOOD-SPATTER INTERPRETATION

CONSIDERATIONS

1) It is critically important in any death scene with blood spatter that the scene be well preserved, that visitors be kept out, and that authorized personnel be allowed into the scene in an orderly, prescribed fashion. A list should be maintained of anyone who accesses the scene.

2) Bloodstain patterns lend themselves to geometric interpretation; it is often possible to analyze the origin of the blood spatter and the mechanics of how the spatter was created and projected.

3) Begin the analysis by searching for blood on items that don't move. Items that move tend to be moved by individuals who have been on the scene. For example, rescue personnel may move a piece of paper found on the floor.

4) The best initial approach to any analysis of the scene based on blood-spatter interpretation is common sense, not expert analysis. In fact, one of the most difficult problems in using the information generated by a blood-spatter analyst is having an "expert" testify to the information; some judges think the information may be given too much weight if an expert testifies. Judges sometimes believe that the members of the jury can look at the same evidence and draw their own conclusions.

QUESTIONS THAT MAY BE ANSWERED WITH BLOOD-SPATTER INTERPRETATION

1) The distance between the target surface and the origin of blood at the time of bloodshed

2) The point(s) of origin of the blood

3) Movement and direction of a person or an object

4) The number of blows, shots, etc., causing the bloodshed or the dispersal of blood

5) Type and direction of impact that produced the bloodshed

6) The position of the victim or object during bloodshed

7) Movement of the victim or object after bloodshed

BLOODSTAIN TERMINOLOGY

(As established by the International Association of Blood Pattern Analysts)

Angle of impact	The angle at which blood strikes a target surface.
Bloodstain	Blood that has come into contact with a surface.
Bloodstain transfer	The patterned blood image left when a bloody object comes into contact with a surface.
Blow-back spatter	Blood that is directed back toward its source of energy. For example, a gunshot fired through a person's head will travel back toward the gun's barrel.
Cast-off bloodstain	Blood that is thrown from an object in motion.
Draw back	The effects of gases on blood involved in a firearm death. The blood is drawn into the barrel of the weapon as the gases cool; this is especially noticeable when the firearm and target are close to each other.
Forward spatter	Blood traveling in the same direction as the force that caused the spatter. It is commonly associated with exit wounds of gunshot victims.
High-force spatter	Blood is subjected to a high-force force greater than 100 fps. It gives the appearance of a fine mist.
Low-force spatter	Blood that has fallen onto a surface at a force of 5 fps or less.
Medium-force spatter	Blood propelled by a medium-force force associated with 5 and 25 fps.
Origin	A point or location where blood originates.
Satellite spatter	Small droplets of blood that are detached from the main blood volume at the moment of its impact with a surface.
Swipe	The transfer of blood onto a surface not already contaminated with blood.
Target	A surface on which blood has been deposited.
Wave cast-off	A blood droplet that is cast off in wavelike action from the originating drop of blood.
Wipe	Where blood has already been deposited on a surface and another object travels through the original bloodstain, removing or depositing blood on this original bloodstain.

SCENE INVESTIGATION

1)   Preserve dried blood.
         a) Suspects may have left dried blood in the form bloody footprints, transfer impressions, including patent prints.

i) Do not step in dried blood. Maintain paths away from areas in which activity obviously took place. If that is not possible, place poster board or butcher paper over areas that may prove to be important.

ii) Use high-intensity lighting to process areas that may hold promise in reconstructing the incident based on blood-spatter interpretation.

iii) Bloodstains can be lifted with tape if deemed necessary for later analysis.
  (1) Use transparent fingerprint tape.
  (2) After carefully photographing the spatter, place the tape over the particular bloodstain. Apply pressure with a closed ballpoint pen or fingernail.
  (3) Peel the tape from the surface. The blood should come up with the tape. Place the tape onto a plastic card (plastic should be used in case access to the spatter is necessary later).

iv) If necessary, remove portions of walls, doors, ceilings, carpeting, etc., for further examination.

v) Look for places blood where should be but isn't.

vi) Obtain all of the victim's and the suspect's clothing.
  (1) Do not bring them in contact with one another.
  (2) Separately bag each item after air-drying it.
  (3) Consider removing victim's clothing prior to transferring decedent from the scene, especially if a significant pattern may be present and in jeopardy of being lost with further pooling or handling. Contact the pathologist responsible for the case for specific approval.
  (4) As a rule of thumb, never bring the suspect to the scene. If there is some compelling reason why he must be brought to the scene, collect his clothing (if he could be wearing the same clothes worn when the crime was committed) prior to letting him enter the scene. Don't forget his shoes.

BLOODSTAIN PHOTOGRAPHY

1) Take distant shots of the blood spatter to reference the bloodstains within a particular area of a particular room. Large scales should be used to cover the surface area in a horizontal and vertical position. Smaller metric scales should be generously placed throughout the spatters for close-up shots.

2) Take intermediate shots of the blood spatter at a 90-degree angle.

3) Take close-up photographs of bloodstains and patterns with a ruler included for perspective.
  a) Photograph at a 90-degree angle to the stain at all times.
  b) Show stain's direction (north, south, east, west) and direction of travel.
    i) Ring-binder reinforcements (do not stick them) may be used to circle high-force spatter along the walls, floors, ceilings, clothing, etc.
  c) When shooting clothing, indicate front and back.

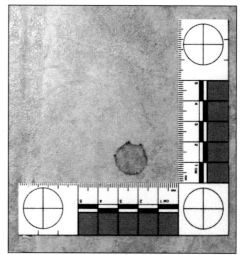

Proper placement of a ruler for a

UNDERSTANDING BLOOD

1)   Perhaps the most important consideration is understanding the importance the surface plays in determining what a blood drop is going to do.

      a) The liquid contained in a blood drop is held together by a cohesive force referred to as *surface tension*. Blood drops as a result of gravity after reaching a uniform volume in an oscillating ball.

            i) If bleeding is rapid, the blood drops may assume a greater volume. If bleeding is slow, the drops will not become smaller.

            ii) If the surface area from which the blood is dropping is small, the volume of the drop may be smaller.

      b) Upon striking a surface, the blood leaves a pattern based on the type of surface it hits. When discussing blood spatter, always identify the surface type.

            i) The harder and less porous the surface, the less the blood drop will break apart. The softer and more porous the surface, the more a blood drop will break apart. For example, blood falling onto smooth glass will remain fairly intact; blood falling onto brushed concrete will tend to break apart.

            ii) The analyst making interpretations concerning properties of blood should make a reference guide indicating where blood has been dropped onto various surfaces at various heights.

SURFACE TYPES

Blood striking
a smooth surface.

Blood striking
a rough surface.

2)   Establish the direction of the bloodstain.

      a) The pointed end of the blood drop faces the direction the stain is traveling.

      b) The "scalloped" edge of the blood drop points in the direction the stain is traveling.

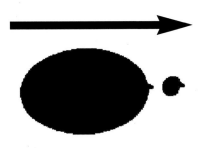

Direction of travel.

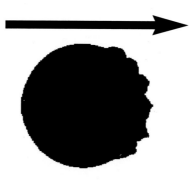

Direction of travel.

c) When blood drop strikes a surface with considerable force and at a rather sharp angle, a smaller droplet, or satellite, is cast off from the larger "parent" drop, much like a breaking wave. This small wave cast-off travels closely to the surface, and in a very short distance begins to streak the surface in a straight line. Usually, this stain appears as a very fine straight line with a rounded end marking the point at which the droplet's forward motion was terminated.

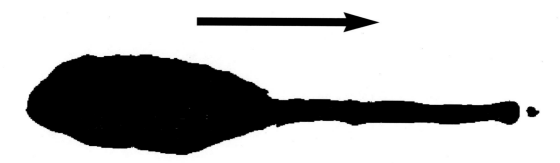

Direction of travel.

3)   When striking a flat surface, the blood spot will assume one of two forms:
        a) Round
                i) A drop of blood falling straight down (90-degree angle) or hitting from straight across onto a flat surface will be geometrically round.
        b) Elliptical
                i) As the angle decreases from 90 degrees to 0 degrees, the blood drop becomes increasingly elongated.
                ii) The angle of a given pattern can be determined fairly simply because there is a mathematical relationship between the shape of the bloodstain and the angle at which it strikes a surface. On a scientific calculator measure the width of the stain, divide by the length of the stain, and hit the arc sine calculator key. This will reveal the angle of the particular pattern.

Width ÷ Length = Sine of the impact angle

4)   The point of origin can be established by placing a protractor on top of the blood drop and running a cord at the indicated angle back toward the direction in which the spatter indicates it came. After running several drops, the cords will cross each other. At the point in which the cords cross, the point of origin for the blood has been established.

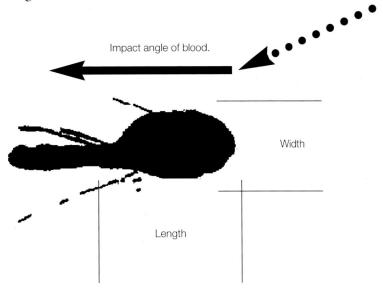

Impact angle of blood.

Width

Length

     a) Interpretation of this convergence indicates to the analyst the height and position the individual likely assumed to have caused the pattern. It may indicate if the victim was standing, sitting in a chair, or lying on a bed. This may supply the investigator with physical facts he needs to refute or confirm an individual's recollection of the events.

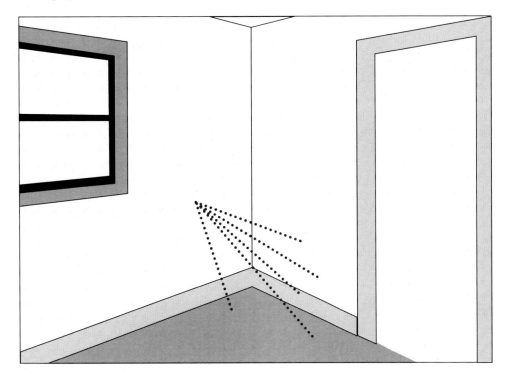

Example of establishing blood convergence based on the spatter.

LOW-FORCE IMPACT SPATTER

1)   This involves blood dripping or being splashed onto a flat surface as a result of a low-energy source acting on the blood at a velocity less than 5 fps. Examples include the following:

        a) Stepping into a pooled area of blood with a foot or shoe. The energy, depending on the force used, may cause the blood to be forced out, away from the pooling. Blood projected up is stopped by the shoe, allowing only the blood to escape from the sides of the foot. Consequently, investigators will see elongated spatter patterns emitting from the pulled area.

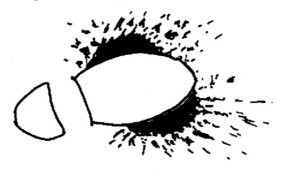

Example of low-force spatter.

        b) Large volumes of blood being flung against the wall or onto the floor are also seen. Most often, these bleeding patterns are produced as a result of a major artery being cut, causing large volumes of blood to be projected in spurts associated with the arterial bleeding. The patterns are often recognized, as they may appear as an EKG chart, especially when the involved person is walking down a hallway or along an area adjacent to walls. In fact, the systolic pressure associated with the heartbeat is likely responsible for this particular pattern. The arteries involved are typically the temporal, carotid, subclavian, and femoral. When the blood from these arteries strikes a flat surface, it is usually seen as follows:

            i) A large volume of splashed blood is characterized by spines or elongated lines resembling a starburst pattern.

Splashed blood.

MEDIUM-FORCE IMPACT SPATTER

1) A blood drop will not break apart while flying through the air unless some type of force acts upon it.

2) The force must have sufficient energy to overcome the surface tension of the blood and thereby release hundreds of smaller droplets. What results is a medium-force spatter.
    a) The diameter of the bloodstains normally exceed 1millimeter, although a considerable number of the bloodstains will be smaller.

3) Impact velocity is between 5 and 25 fps. This is normally associated with beating-type injuries, especially those beatings in which a blunt object is used.
    a) Shotgun shots to bloody heads notwithstanding, any occasion in which an expansive area is covered with blood, initial consideration should be given to a beating death involving multiple blows to the head.
        i) If a particular void is observed in a blood-covered scene, the void tends to indicate that an intermediate target was present. That is, someone or something was present at the scene during bloodshed and has been subsequently removed from the scene.
        ii) Suspects responsible for the beatings will often, but not always, become the target of the some of the blood spatter. The suspect's clothing should become a focal point for the investigator because it may reveal certain spatters that are consistent with medium-force spatter consistent with the beating death.
            (1) Placing ring-binder type of paper reinforcements (do not lick them) around each area of spatter on the clothing and photographing this spatter is an excellent way to demonstrate this evidence.

HIGH-FORCE SPATTER

1) This involves a greater force applied to the liquid blood, breaking it into much finer particles. The mass of blood atomizes, causing the blood to be in an aerosol or fine-mist form.
    a) Because the blood is converted into this fine, mist-like spray, it will not travel very far unless influenced by some external force, such as an open door or a breeze.

2) Typical examples of high-force spatter include, but are not limited to, gunshots, explosions, and individuals who may have walked into a propeller or other machinery involving high revolutions of parts.

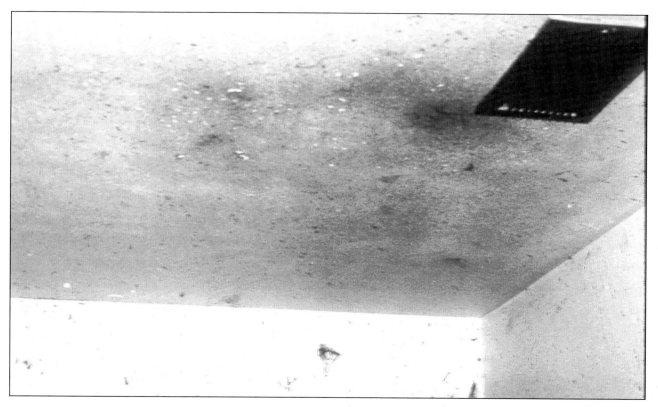

Example of high-force spatter (shotgun wound to the head) on the ceiling.

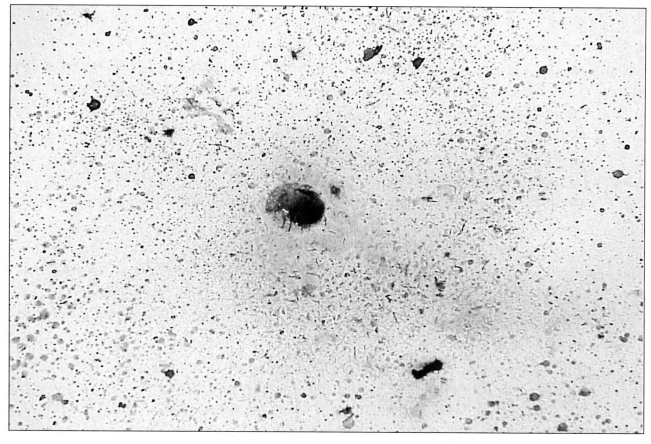

High-force spatter.

Through-and-through gunshot wound to the head.

3)   Through-and-through gunshot wounds to the head produce two sources of blood:
        a) The entrance wound causes blood to be dispersed back toward the barrel of the
           weapon (blow-back spatter, in-shoot). Examine for patterns of blood on the hands of
           the decedent (suicide), hands of the suspect, and in the barrel of the suspected weapon.
        b) High-force spatter, brain, tissue, and bone accompany the exiting projectile.

CAST-OFF BLOODSTAIN SPATTERS

1)   Cast-off spatters involve blood projected by an object in motion. It is normally associated with at
        least two blows: the first blow produces the blood; the second blow (and all subsequent blows)
        disperses it as the blood adheres to instrument used.
        a) If the instrument used to effect the beating retains blood very well, a downward-
           directed trail may also be visible because the bloodied instrument casts off a pattern on
           the downward stroke prior to striking the victim an additional time.

2)   A distinctive trail (or trails) will lead away from the body or point of convergence.
        a) To determine the number of blows, count the number of distinctive trails.

3)   Blood present on the ceiling usually indicates cast-off spatter. The area under the ceiling where
        perpendicular spatter is observed is normally associated with the site where the attack took place.
        The farther away from the attack, the more elongated the spatter becomes.
        a) If the victim moved around during the beating, multiple areas of perpendicular
           spatters will be observed on the ceiling.

EXPIRATED BLOOD

1)   Sometimes incorrectly called *aspirated blood*, expirated blood refers to blood that has collected in
        the victim's airway and gets blown out through the nose and/or mouth. It may appear as a
        medium- or high-force area of spatter.

2)   The best ways to determine whether spatter was produced by expirated blood rather than a medium- or high-force impact are these:

   a) Determine whether blood is present in the nose or mouth of the victim. If it is not present, this is not the source of the spatter.
   b) Determine whether the area in which the spatter appears could have been in the relative area of the nose and mouth to receive the spatter.

TRANSFER BLOODSTAIN PATTERNS

1)   Transferring bloodstain patterns involves the transfer of geometric images onto items or areas that

do not contain blood. It can involve transfers of:

   a) Finger and palm prints
   b) Shoe prints
   c) Weapons, including knives, metal bars, baseball bats, tire irons, etc.

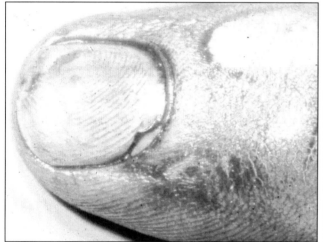

A bloody fingerprint was left behind on the victim's fingernail by the killer.

A bloody knife's impression is outlined in blood.

   d) Hair swipe patterns involving a victim's hair normally seen as a feather-edged and fine-lined transfer blood pattern.

2)   Interpretations of transfer blood patterns are sometimes critical to a case. For example, an examination of a person's clothing may indicate that *projected* blood is found within the recesses of the fabrics, not the *transfer* blood that should be present in the higher points of the fabric weave only. This could mean the subject did not get the blood when brushing up against the victim, as he claimed, but rather had to be present at a time in which the blood was being projected.

BLOODSTAIN AS A TIMING MECHANISM

1)   Tests can be conducted to determine general drying times involving general amounts of blood present on specific surfaces. These tests are generally so ambiguous that any conclusions may lend themselves to severe criticism.

BLOODSTAIN SEQUENCE

1) Blood spatter that falls on top of other spatter patterns may be able to provide analysts with a sequence for particular events to have occurred.

    a) A commonly seen occurrence is referred to as a "skeletal" outline of blood patterns. These are caused because the outside periphery of the stain will dry before the inner core. Before the drying process can become complete, someone touches the spatter, causing the center of the spatter to be removed and leaving the previously dried, doughnut-looking outline behind.

CREATING A BLOOD KIT

1) The following items should be collected to help the investigator interpret blood patterns:

Metric ruler	12-inch ruler
L-shaped ruler	Adhesive metric stickers
Protractor with cord attached	Ball of cord
Tape measure	Flashlight
Magnifying glass	Presumptive field test for blood
Metal stands used to run convergence patterns	Narrow widths of various colored tapes
Binder-type reinforcements	Adhesive rulers used in connecting horizontal and vertical increments

PRESUMPTIVE BLOOD TESTING OF SUSPECTED BLOOD

1) For the detection of blood on specific items, in trace amounts, most labs use the Kastle-Meyer Reagent (Phenolphthalein) Presumptive Blood Test.

    a) Advantages

        i) Highly sensitive

        ii) Does not contaminate blood typing

        iii) Comparatively specific

        iv) Easily portable

        v) Easy to use

        vi) Immediate deep vivid pink chemical reaction indicating presumptive blood

        vii) Recognized in courts around the world as a presumptive test for blood

        viii) Use as a prelaboratory test for blood

    b) Materials

        i) Phenolphthalein, 2 grams

        ii) Sodium hydroxide, 20 grams

        iii) Zinc dust, 20 grams

        iv) Distilled water, 500 milliliters

        v) The mixture is refluxed until colorless and then cooled.

        vi) Hydrogen peroxide

vii) Ethyl alcohol
c) Techniques
    i) On suspected dried bloodstains, moisten a swab with distilled water.
    ii) Rub swab lightly on a stain.
    iii) Deposit one drop of ethyl alcohol on swab surface.
    iv) Deposit one drop of reagent on swab surface.
    v) Deposit one drop of hydrogen peroxide on swab surface.
d) Reaction
    i) An immediate deep vivid pink coloration indicates a positive reaction.
e) Drawbacks
    i) The test is presumptive for blood.
    ii) When aging, phenolphthalein will turn pink when wet.
    iii) The chemicals will break down in heat after 6 months. It is necessary to keep the mixture cool.
    iv) It is too costly to spray over large areas.

LUMINOL USE

1) If you suspect that the blood patterns on walls, furniture, clothing, and carpeting have been cleaned, a chemical application of luminol may reproduce the original pattern.

2) Luminol is best used for the detection of traces of blood that are not readily observable at crime scenes.

3) The sensitivity of the luminol test is as high as approximately 1 part in 5 million.

4) Luminol works very well with aged and decomposed bloodstains.
    a) Luminol uses certain chemicals that luminesce the iron oxides of blood that may remain in suspected material, even after cleanup has occurred.

5) Procedure for use
    a) Locate suspected stains.
        i) This includes light tracking of blood on dark floors and carpeted areas, cracks and crevices in floors and walls, and areas where an attempt to clean bloodstained areas is suspected.
        ii) The patterns of blood revealed with luminol may be as important as the detection of blood itself.
    b) Perform a field presumptive blood test.
        i) Preferences for the type of the field presumptive serological testing of luminol should be obtained from the forensic laboratory associated with the involved agency.
    c) If presumptive field test is positive, luminol the item.
    d) A bluish-white luminescence or light on the suspected area observed in the dark is a positive test.
    e) Take photographs of the luminol reaction.

6) Advantages of using luminol
    a) Since it is applied as a spray, large areas can be covered.
    b) It reveals bloodstains unseen by the naked eye in such detail that it allows for patterns to be interpreted, for example:

　　　　i) Drag marks
　　　　ii) Swipe marks
　　　　iii) Tracks
　　　　iv) Hand impressions
　　　　v) Low-, medium-, and high-force impact spatters
　　c) Photographs can be taken of the process results and used for court presentations.
　　d) It is an excellent investigative and interrogative tool.
　　e) Luminol is legally and scientifically accepted in many states.

7)　　There are several distinct disadvantages to using luminol.
　　a) It will react with certain vegetable peroxides, chemicals, and metals, for example:
　　　　i) Bronze
　　　　ii) Brass
　　　　iii) All metals containing copper
　　　　iv) Grease and some oils containing trace amounts of copper
　　　　v) Some vegetable peroxide, including horseradish, potato, turnip, cabbage, onion, dandelion root, apple, apricot, bean, blackberry, and Jerusalem artichoke
　　　　vi) Some ceramic tiles and grout
　　　　vii) Rust (on some occasions)
　　　　viii) Formalin, potassium permanganate, hydrated sodium, and hypochlorite
　　　　ix) Pus, bone marrow, leukocytes, brain tissue, spinal fluid, intestine, lung, saliva, and mucous.
　　b) Try not to luminol the item more than twice: any blood that might be on a sprayed object may dissolve in the solution.
　　c) Photographing the luminol reaction takes some photographic sophistication.

8)　　Photographic considerations associated with luminol use
　　a) Luminol photography is used in the detection of blood and bloodstains related to evidence because it is highly sensitive and capable of being used for blood detection where blood has been diluted.
　　b) Photos require time exposures during diminished depth-of-field situations in which the photography is conducted in near-total darkness.
　　c) ISO should not exceed 400. Aperture setting should be at least f/2.8.
　　d) The following equipment is suggested for the use and photographic documentation of luminol fluorescence:
　　　　i) Luminol reagent and spraying device
　　　　ii) Black plastic cover for bottle housing during test
　　　　iii) Luminescent measuring device
　　　　iv) Camera, normal standard lens, B (bulb) shutter setting, and wide-open lens setting f/2.8 or more.
　　　　　　(1) SLR camera a 55mm lens for footprints and a wide-angle lens such as 35mm for scene shots
　　　　　　(2) Manual cameras, which are less likely to fail during timed exposures
　　　　v) Shutter release cable
　　　　vi) Tripod
　　　　　　(1) Extension arm useful
　　　　vii) Flash unit
　　　　viii) ASA 400 black and white or color film
　　　　　　(1) Examples of film used
　　　　　　　　(a) Kodak Vericolor 400 or HC, Konica super XG400).

(b) Ilford 400 ASA XP2 black and white film, giving excellent footprint impressions
  ix) Timer
    (1) An audible, luminous dark room clock for timing long exposures may be necessary.
  x) Appropriate protective clothing: gloves, coveralls, and goggles
e) Photographing footprints requires the following:
  i) Angle finder
  ii) A set square, preferably with white, recessed graduation marks (the white recesses will fill up with luminol reagent and emit a fluorescent scale in the photographs)
f) Marking areas of interest at the scene will require the following:
  i) White chalk
  ii) Adhesive fluorescent markers
  iii) Sketch pad and pen
  iv) Flashlight

9)   Luminol photography method
    a) Two to three crime scene officers may be required for this procedure:
      i) One sprays the luminol.
      ii) A second operates the camera.
      iii) A third operates the timer and lights.
    b) Prior to the use of the luminol reagent, the surface or object should be photographed in position using a flash unit with the luminescent ruler in place.
      i) This will be helpful in subsequent examinations of the photos to establish the location of the positive luminescent areas as it will appear on a dark background.
    c) A camera holder using two cameras at the same time is gaining popularity among crime scene technicians.
    d) Always keep the camera lens perpendicular to the subject surface except when shooting the overall views.
    e) The camera lens f/stop should then be set at the widest aperture and the exposure setting at the B (bulb) position.
    f) Attach the shutter cable release.
    g) With the room or location darkened, apply the luminol reagent with the spraying device using a slow, even motion to avoid saturating the sprayed surface.
      i) Use as fine a mist as possible.
      ii) The surface can be resprayed during the time exposure to enhance the reaction.
    h) An exposure time of 90 seconds should be suitable and produce satisfactory results. If a second camera is used, the exposure will continue for an additional 30 seconds (2 minutes total). The final second of exposure on the 2-minute exposure should be used to bounce the light from a flashlight up toward the ceiling for just a split second. This will allow identifying features in the room to be visualized in the photograph in comparison to the luminol exposure.
      i) Before shooting the subject material, practice with the timing of the exposure.

10)   Using luminol on footprints and suspected stains
    a) Lightly spray luminol solution on the target areas to locate bloodstains and footprint impressions.

b) Discontinue the spraying when impressions or stains are detected.

c) Place the set square scale next to the impression.

d) Place a white piece of paper bearing the exhibit number in thick, bold, black letters and numbers alongside the scale so that it is included in the photograph.

    i) The white graduation marks should react with the luminol and provide a scale on your photograph.

e) Switch the lights on and position your tripod and camera over the target area.

f) Focus and use your angle finder to ensure that the camera is parallel in lateral and horizontal planes with respect to the target.

g) With the lights switched on, take a normal exposure.

    i) This can be used for reference purposes if scaling problems are encountered during the production of 1:1 photograph prints.

h) Set the aperture to its widest setting to let the maximum amount of light into the camera.

    i) Timed exposures of between 3.5 to 5 minutes have provided good-quality negatives and good resolution of gauging and markers.

i) Set the timer.

j) Switch off the lights while spraying the luminol solution over the target area.

    i) Spray enough solution to give the strongest luminescence.

    ii) Excessive spraying can actually reduce the intensity.

k) Open the camera shutter with the cable release.

l) Repeat the spraying when the luminescence dies down.

m) After 5 minutes close the shutter and turn on the lights.

11) Using luminol on large scene areas

a) If a large area is to be tested during one application, then a garden-type sprayer may be better suited as an applicator.

    i) Photographs of this larger area may be necessary to demonstrate drag marks, footprints throughout this particular area, spatter, etc.

    ii) Fluorescent markers and chalk to mark relevant findings may be used.

b) A useful photographic technique involves photographing the luminol-treated subject in total darkness but with the addition of a small amount of light to give a minimal image of the subject or area.

    i) This can be accomplished by firing a flashgun in the corner of the room or at the ceiling (bounce flash) during the timed exposure.

ENHANCEMENT OF SHOE PRINTS IN BLOOD THROUGH THE USE OF LEUCOCRYSTAL VIOLET

1) Leucocrystal violet (LCV)

a) LCV is considered a better alternative than the more commonly used choices for enhancement of bloody footwear impressions including Amido Black, diaminobenzidine (DAB), and luminol.

    i) Luminol has been used frequently in cases where the background colors of the object would interfere with Amido Black or DAB, or in those cases where it would not be feasible to use Amido Black or DAB.

    ii) Negatives associated with using luminol

        (1) Luminol is very sensitive to blood and because it is applied in total darkness, the object's background color does not interfere with visualization of the impression. However, the choice of luminol is

accompanied by other restrictions, such as the large amount of time needed for luminol processing and the difficulty of photography in total darkness.

(2) Prior to luminol processing, a screening of the entire floor surface is necessary to specifically identify the location of each impression so that close-up examination-quality photographs can be taken. Luminol photography of large areas, as with a general crime-scene photograph, would not provide the necessary detail for examination, and, due to the photographic law of inverse proportions, may not adequately result in exposure of all impressions and therefore could result in the loss of evidence.

b) Visible bloody impressions on porous items (e.g., paper, wood, fabric and medium- to dark-blue carpeting) are best processed with DAB and, if needed, followed with Amido Black.

c) LCV is particularly effective in processing large areas where many latent footwear impressions may be present.

i) It is far more convenient and versatile than luminol and allows for better observations of the footwear impressions since it is applied and viewed in existing ambient light.

ii) ALS, specialized photography of developed impressions, and subsequent treatment with Amido Black can enhance detail for comparison.

2)   Creating a working solution

a) Dissolve 10 grams of 5-sulphosalicylic acid (Sigma # S-2130) in 500 milliliters of 3-percent hydrogen peroxide.

b) Add and dissolve 4.4 grams of sodium acetate.

c) Add and dissolve 1.1 grams of LCV (Sigma # L-5760) (use a magnetic stirrer)

d) NOTE: If LCV crystals have become yellow instead of white, discard and get fresh crystals.

e) After the solution is mixed it should be stored in dark-colored glassware and refrigerated. It will last several months.

3)   Application

a) The application of LCV, particularly to large-crime-scene areas in most scenarios, has several distinct advantages over Amido Black, DAB, and luminol.

i) It is easy to mix and, with reasonable safety precautions, does not present any significant health hazards.

ii) It results in almost instant visualization of impressions, which in turn enables that information to be incorporated in photographs, crime-scene notes, and sketches.

(1) If further improved visualization is needed, the area containing the impressions can be removed from the scene to the laboratory, where specialized photography and further enhancement with the Amido Black may be performed.

b) 5-sulphosalicylic acid fixes the blood; therefore, the solution may be directly applied to the impression area in one step.

i) Applications of LCV may be made by lightly spraying with an aerosol device or by immersion. The reaction takes place rapidly.

ii) Where the LCV clear solution comes into contact with blood, the blood impression turns a purple/violet color, instantly providing improved visualization.

(1) When LCV and hydrogen peroxide come into contact with the hemoglobin in blood, a catalytic reaction occurs and causes the solution to turn a purple/violet color.

c) Overspraying with LCV may discolor some objects in time because of photoionization.

    i) Individual impressions that are detected can be removed from the scene.

    ii) Subsequent processing with Amido Black methanol/glacial acetic acid formulation will further enhance the impression and eliminate most discoloration.

4)   Sequencing

    a) After treatment of a bloody impression with LCV

        i) Use conventional black and white photography. Proper filtration may be necessary to negate the background color of the object.

        ii) Consideration should be given to using either visible fluorescence and/or infrared luminescence for enhancement of the print.

    b) After applying LCV, methanol/glacial acetic acid, Amido Black stain formulation may be applied for further enhancement of the print.

        i) LCV cannot follow nor be followed by DAB.

    c) LCV can be applied following luminol treatment of bloodstains. However, if this sequence is used, it is necessary to first fix the stain with a 2-percent 5-sulphosalicylic acid solution prior to the luminol treatment, since luminol treatment without fixation causes significant leaching and loss of detail.

BLOOD-SPATTER IMPACT CHART

		90° Perpendicular Spatter 17x17mm
		80° 17x16.5 mm
		70° 17x16 mm
		60° 17x15mm

BLOOD-SPATTER IMPACT CHART

		50° 17x14.5mm
		40° 18x12mm
		30° 22x11mm

BLOOD-SPATTER IMPACT CHART

		20° 20x7mm
		10° 43x7mm

SOURCES OF ARTERIAL BLEEDING

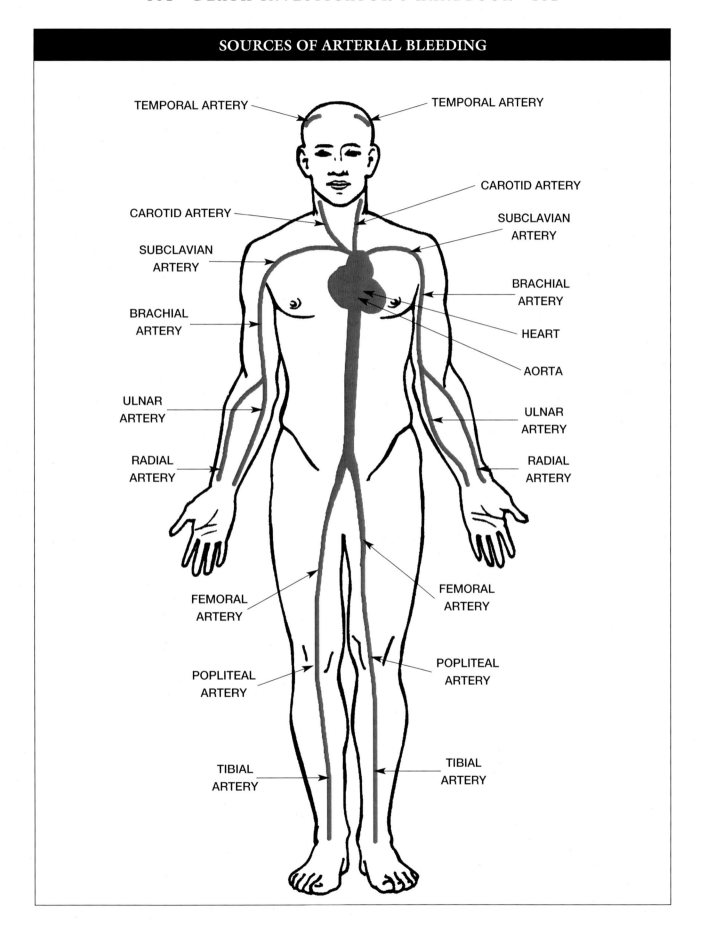

NOTE: This index is found in the back of all three volumes. Pages 1–132 appear in Volume 1; pages 133–648 in Volume 2; pages 649–976 in Volume 3.

I

M

P

ABOUT THE AUTHOR

Louis N. Eliopulos has 25 years of experience in death investigations. Currently, he is a senior homicide investigations analyst with the Naval Criminal Investigative Service (NCIS), where he reviews, consults, and suggests investigative analysis and strategy on active and cold-case homicide investigations from all over the world. He also consults on homicide investigations for other criminal justice agencies. Before being employed by NCIS, Eliopulos was chief forensic investigator for the Medical Examiner's Office in Jacksonville, Florida, where he created, hired and trained the investigative staff, as well as serving as the special investigator in the Capital Crimes Division for the Florida Public Defender's Office. He also was a forensic consultant for the teams responsible for recovering the remains from the Pentagon after the September 11, 2001, terrorist attack.

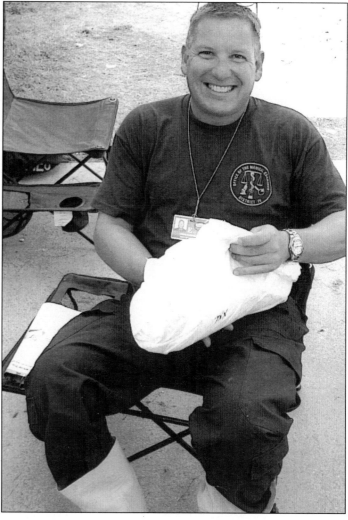